Federal Benefits for Veterans, Dependents, Survivors, and Caregivers

You are not alone.

Confidential crisis support is available 24/7.

Chat at VeteransCrisisLine.net/Chat
Text 838255

Federal Benefits for Veterans, Dependents, Survivors, and Caregivers

2025 Edition

US DEPARTMENT OF VETERANS AFFAIRS

Skyhorse Publishing

The 2025 Federal Benefits for Veterans, Dependents, Survivors, and Caregivers provides information on benefits and services currently available by law and regulation. The information provided in the guide was validated by VA as of October 10, 2024. Go to va.gov to access the latest updates on Veteran care and benefits.

All rights reserved. No part of this book may be reproduced in any manner without the express written consent of the publisher, except in the case of brief excerpts in critical reviews or articles. All inquiries should be addressed to Skyhorse Publishing, 307 West 36th Street, 11th Floor, New York, NY 10018.

Skyhorse Publishing books may be purchased in bulk at special discounts for sales promotion, corporate gifts, fund-raising, or educational purposes. Special editions can also be created to specifications. For details, contact the Special Sales Department, Skyhorse Publishing, 307 West 36th Street, 11th Floor, New York, NY 10018 or info@skyhorsepublishing.com.

Skyhorse® and Skyhorse Publishing® are registered trademarks of Skyhorse Publishing, Inc.®, a Delaware corporation.

Visit our website at www.skyhorsepublishing.com.
Please follow our publisher Tony Lyons on Instagram @tonylyonsisuncertain.

10 9 8 7 6 5 4 3 2 1

Library of Congress Cataloging-in-Publication Data is available on file.

Cover design by Kai Texel

Print ISBN: 978-1-5107-8321-8
Ebook ISBN: 978-1-5107-8322-5

Printed in the United States of America

Federal Benefits for Veterans, Dependents, Survivors, and Caregivers | i

Phone Numbers

Veterans Crisis Line ....Dial 988, then Press 1

VA Hotline ....800-MyVA411 (800-698-2411, option 9)

MyVA411...800-698-2411

Bereavement Counseling (through Vet Centers) 877-927-8387

Camp Lejeune Family Member Program 866-372-1144

Civilian Health and Medical Program (CHAMPVA) 800-733-8387
Community Care Billing Questions...877-881-7618

Debt Management Center 800-827-0648

Education 888-442-4551

Foreign Medical Program . ...877-345-8179 or 303-331-7590

Headstones and Markers..800-697-6947

Health Care 877-222-8387

Homeless Veterans..877-424-3838

Home Loans 877-827-3702

Life Insurance, All Programs Other than SGLI, FSGLI,
TSGLI, VGLI 800-669-8477

Life Insurance, Veterans' Group Life Insurance Program (VGLI),
Claims for Service members' Group Life Insurance (SGLI)
and Family SGLI...800-419-1473

National Cemetery Scheduling Office 800-535-1117

Native American Direct Home Loans 888-349-7541

Presidential Memorial Certificate Program 202-565-4964

Spina Bifida Program..888-820-1756

TTY, Federal Relay...711

VA Benefits...800-827-1000

Vet Center Call Center..877-927-8387

Women Veterans..877-222-8387

72-Hour Emergency Care Notification Line 844-724-7842

Websites

VA Home Page .... www.VA.gov

Benefits and Services Overview .... www.choose.va.gov

Burial and Memorial Benefits .... www.cem.va.gov

Caregiver Support .... www.caregiver.va.gov

Center for Minority Veterans .... www.va.gov/centerforminorityveterans

CHAMPVA .... www.va.gov/communitycare/programs/dependents/champva

Community Care .... www.va.gov/communitycare

Dental Care .... www.va.gov/dental

Disability Claims and Appeals .... www.va.gov/claim-or-appeal-status

Education Benefits .... www.va.gov/education

Environmental Exposures .... www.publichealth.va.gov/exposures

Federal Recovery Consultant Office .... www.va.gov/vadodhealth/frcp.asp

Geriatrics and Extended Care .... www.va.gov/geriatrics

Health Care Eligibility .... www.va.gov/health-care

Homeless Veterans .... www.va.gov/homeless

Home Loan Guaranty .... www.benefits.va.gov/homeloans

Life Insurance .... www.benefits.va.gov/insurance

Memorial Certificate Program .... www.cem.va.gov/pmc.asp

Mental Health .... www.mentalhealth.va.gov

My HealtheVet .... www.myhealth.va.gov

National Resource Directory .... www.nrd.gov

PACT Act .... www.VA.gov/PACT

Federal Benefits for Veterans, Dependents, Survivors, and Caregivers | iii

Post 9/11 Veterans www.va.gov/post911veterans

Transitioning Service members .... benefits.va.gov/transition/tap.asp

Service Records .... www.archives.gov/personnel-records-center/military-personnel

State Departments of Veterans Affairs .... www.va.gov/statedva.htm

Welcome Kit... www.va.gov/welcome-kit

Women Veterans.. www.womenshealth.va.gov

.... www.benefits.va.gov/persona/veteran-women.asp

.... www.va.gov/womenvet

VA Forms .... www.va.gov/vaforms

VA Health Connect... mobile.va.gov/app/va-health-chat

VA Solid Start .... www.benefits.va.gov/transition/solid-start.asp

VA Vet Centers .... www.vetcenter.va.gov

Veteran & Military Spouse Talent Engagement Program (VMSTEP)........................... www.vaforvets.va.gov

Veteran Readiness and Employment .... www.va.gov/careers-employment/vocational-rehabilitation

Veterans Crisis Line .... www.veteranscrisisline.net

VHA Notice of Privacy Practices........... www.va.gov/vhapublications/ViewPublication.asp?pub_ID=9946

72-Hour Emergency Care Notification Portal........ emergencycarereporting.communitycare.va.gov/request

Legal Status and Use of Seals and Logos

The seal of the Department of Veterans Affairs authenticates the 2025 edition of Federal Benefits for Veterans, Dependents Survivors and Caregivers as the official summary of benefits that have been separately promulgated under Federal regulations established under Register Act. Under the provisions of 38 Code of Federal Regulations 1.9(f), it is prohibited to use the official seal, replicas, reproductions, or embossed seals of the Department of Veterans Affairs on any republication of this material without the express, written permission of the Secretary or Deputy Secretary of Veterans Affairs. Any person using official seals and logos of the Department of Veterans Affairs in a manner inconsistent with the provisions of 38 Code of Federal Regulations 1.9 may be subject to the penalties specified in 18 United States Code 506, 701, or 1017 as applicable.

Contents

Phone Numbers i

Websites ii

Introduction 1

Health Care 3
  Eligibility and Enrollment 3
  How to Apply for VA Health Care 4
  VA Health Care Programs and Services 7
  Emergency Medical Care in U.S. Community Facilities 10
  Urgent Care in U.S. Community Facilities 11

Non-Health Care Benefits 27
  Disabled Veterans 27

Veteran Readiness and Employment 33

Pension 37

Education and Training 40

Home Loans 47

Life Insurance 56

Re-Employment Rights 64

Homelessness Assistance and Prevention 65

Family Members/Survivors 69

Appeals and Supplemental Claims 75

Burial and Memorial Benefits 81
  Burial in VA National Cemeteries 81
  Other Memorialization 87

Additional Benefits 92

Attention Veterans, Family Members, Survivors, and Caregivers

The 2025 Federal Benefits Guide for Veterans, Dependents, Survivors, and Caregivers provides information on benefits and services currently available by law and regulation. The information provided in the guide is validated by VA as of Oct 10, 2024. Please go to va.gov to access the latest updates on Veteran care and benefits.

On August 10, 2022, the Sergeant First Class Heath Robinson Honoring our Promise to Address Comprehensive Toxics Act of 2022, referred to as the PACT Act, was signed into law. The law expands VA health care and benefits for Veterans exposed to burn pits and other toxic substances, providing generations of Veterans—and their survivors—with the care and benefits they have earned and deserve. The enactment of the PACT Act marks the largest expansion of VA benefits in 30 years. Learn more about the PACT Act by visiting www.VA.gov/PACT or by calling 800-MY-VA-411.

On June 7, 2022, the Dr. Kate Hendricks Thomas Supporting Expanded Review for Veterans in Combat Environments Act, referred to as the SERVICE Act, was signed into law. The law expands eligibility for breast cancer risk assessments by a VA health care provider and mammography screening when clinically appropriate for Veterans who deployed during active military, naval, or air service to an identified area where they may have had a toxic exposure, such as from burn pits.

On December 29, 2022, the Joseph Maxwell Cleland and Robert Joseph Dole Memorial Veterans Benefits and Health Care Improvement Act (Cleland-Dole Act; Division U of P.L. 117-328) expanded eligibility for VA health care and nursing home care to Veterans of World War II. Unless eligible for a higher priority group, World War II Veterans will be enrolled in Priority Group 6 and be copayment exempt for any care and medications related to their service. However, these Veterans may still have to pay a modest copayment for medication, urgent care, or long-term care in some cases, depending on their eligibility and service connection.

On April 4, 2023, VA adopted a Final Rule exempting Indian and Urban Indian Veterans from copayments for hospital care or medical services, including urgent care visits, received on or after January 5, 2022.

Introduction

Veterans of the United States (U.S.) Armed Forces may be eligible for a broad range of benefits and services provided by the U.S. Department of Veterans Affairs (VA). These benefits are codified in Title 38 of the United States Code (U.S.C.). This booklet contains overviews of the most commonly sought information about Veterans' benefits and services. For the most up-to-date information, Veterans and family members should visit the websites provided within this publication as regulations, payments, and eligibility requirements are subject to change. For additional information, please visit www.va.gov. To find the nearest VA facility, go to www.va.gov/find-locations. As a companion to the booklet, the VA Welcome Kit is available at www.va.gov/welcome-kit/ to explore VA benefits and services more in-depth.

General Eligibility: Eligibility for most VA benefits is based on discharge from active military service under other than dishonorable conditions. Active service means full-time service, other than active duty for training, as a member of the Army, Navy, Air Force, Marine Corps, Coast Guard, Space Force or as a commissioned officer of the Public Health Service, Environmental Science Services Administration, or National Oceanic and Atmospheric Administration, or its predecessor, the Coast and Geodetic Survey. Dishonorable and bad conduct discharges issued by general court-martial may bar Veterans from receiving VA benefits. Veterans in prison must contact VA to determine eligibility. VA benefits will not be provided to any Veteran or dependent with an outstanding felony warrant.

Eligible Wartime Periods: Certain VA benefits require wartime service. For more information on eligible wartime periods, please visit www.va.gov/pension/eligibility/.

Important Documents: Veterans seeking VA benefits for the first time can submit a copy of their service discharge form (DD-214, DD-215 or for some World War II Veterans, a WD form), which documents the Veteran's service dates and the type of discharge. These documents are received upon release from active duty and provide the Veteran's full name, military service number, branch, and dates of service. The Veteran's service discharge form should always be kept in a safe location accessible to the Veteran's next

2 | Introduction

of kin or representative. If you do not provide a copy of your discharge form, VA will make every effort to obtain it on your behalf and will notify you if we are unable to do so.

To process a claim pertaining to the death of a Veteran, the following documents may be required: Veteran's marriage certificate; Veteran's death certificate if the Veteran did not die in a VA health care facility; children's birth certificates or adoption papers; or Veteran's birth certificate.

For information and updates on VA benefits and services, follow us on Facebook at www.facebook.com/VeteransBenefits and X at Veterans Benefits (@VAVetBenefits) / X.

Health Care

Eligibility and Enrollment

The following resources provide detailed information about VA health care, including answers to frequently asked questions: www.va.gov/health-care/ and toll-free at 877-222-VETS (877-222-8387), Monday through Friday between 8 a.m. and 8 p.m. ET., or 1-800-MyVA411 (800-698-2411), option 2.

Basic Eligibility: A person who served in the active military, naval, space or air service, and who was discharged or released under conditions other than dishonorable, including qualifying Reserve and National Guard members, may qualify for VA health care benefits.

Minimum Duty Requirements: Veterans who enlisted after September 7, 1980, or who entered active duty after October 16, 1981, must have served 24-continuous months or the full period for which they were called to active duty to be eligible. This minimum duty requirement may not apply to Veterans discharged for hardship, early out or a disability incurred or aggravated in the line of duty, or those accessing care under certain special treatment authorities, such as treatment related to military sexual trauma (MST).

Returning Service members: Veterans who served in a theater of operations after November 11, 2001, are eligible for an extended period of eligibility for health care for ten years after their discharge. In the case of multiple call-ups, the ten-year enrollment period begins on the most recent discharge date. This special eligibility includes cost-free health care services and nursing home care for conditions possibly related to military service and enrollment in priority group 6 or higher for ten years from their date of discharge or release from active duty, unless they are eligible for enrollment in a higher priority group.

The following four categories of Veterans are not required to enroll, but are urged to do so to permit better planning of health resources:

4 | Health Care

- Veterans with a service-connected disability rated at 50% or more.

- Veterans seeking care for a disability the military determined was incurred or aggravated in the line of duty, but which VA has not yet rated, within 12 months of discharge.

- Veterans seeking care for a service-connected disability only, or under a special treatment authority, such as for treatment related to MST.

- Veterans seeking registry examinations (ionizing radiation, Agent Orange, Gulf War/Operation Enduring Freedom/ Operation Iraqi Freedom/Operation New Dawn (OEF/OIF/ OND) depleted uranium, airborne hazards, and Open Burn Pit Registry).

How to Apply for VA Health Care

Veterans can complete applications for enrollment in VA health care using one of the options below:

- To apply by phone, call 877-222-VETS (877-222-8387) Monday through Friday between 8 a.m. and 8 p.m. ET., or 1-800-MyVA411 (800-698-2411), option 2. VA staff will collect the needed information and process the application for an enrollment determination.

- When applying online at www.va.gov/health-care/apply/ application/introduction Veterans fill out the application and electronically submit it to VA for processing. VA will search for your supporting documentation through its electronic information systems and contact you if VA staff cannot verify your military service.

- The application form can also be downloaded from www. va.gov/health-care/apply/application/introduction. Mail the completed form to: Health Eligibility Center, ATTN: Enrollment Eligibility Division, PO Box 5207, Janesville, WI 53547-5207.

- Veterans can also apply in person at most VA medical centers and some clinics. To find a facility near you, go to www. va.gov/find-locations/.

Once enrolled, Veterans can receive health care at VA health care facilities anywhere in the country.

Priority Groups: During enrollment, each Veteran is assigned to a priority group. VA uses priority groups to balance the demand for VA health care enrollment with resources. Changes in available resources may reduce the number of priority groups VA can enroll. If this occurs, VA will publicize the changes and notify affected enrollees. A description of priority groups follows:

Group 1: Veterans with service-connected disabilities rated 50% or more; Veterans determined by VA to be unemployable due to service-connected conditions; and Veterans who have been awarded the Medal of Honor.

Group 2: Veterans with service-connected disabilities rated 30 or 40%.

Group 3: Veterans who are former prisoners of war (POW); Veterans awarded the Purple Heart medal; Veterans whose discharge was for a disability incurred or aggravated in the line of duty; Veterans with VA service-connected disabilities rated by VA at 10 or 20%; Veterans whose disability compensation is suspended because of the receipt of military retired pay; Veterans receiving compensation at the 10% rate based on multiple non-compensable service-connected disabilities that clearly interfere with normal employability; and Veterans awarded special eligibility classification under Title 38, U.S.C., § 1151, "benefits for individuals disabled by treatment or vocational rehabilitation."

Group 4: Veterans who receive increased compensation or pension based on their need for regular aid and attendance or by reason of being permanently housebound and Veterans determined by VA to be catastrophically disabled.

Group 5: Nonservice-connected Veterans and non- compensable service-connected Veterans rated by VA as 0% disabled and who have an annual income below the VA's geographically adjusted income limit (based on Veteran's ZIP code); Veterans receiving VA Pension benefits; and Veterans eligible for Medicaid benefits.

6 | Health Care

Group 6: Compensable 0% service-connected Veterans; Veterans exposed to ionizing radiation during atmospheric testing or during the occupation of Hiroshima and Nagasaki; Project 112/SHAD participants; World War II (WW II) Veterans; Veterans who served in the Republic of Vietnam between January 9, 1962, and May 7, 1975; toxic exposed Veterans who served in specific locations during certain periods; Veterans who served in the Southwest Asia theater of operations from August 2, 1990, through November 11, 1998; and Veterans who served in a theater of combat operations after November 11, 1998, as follows: Veterans discharged from active duty on or after September 11, 2001, for ten years post discharge; and Veterans who served on active duty at Marine Corps Base Camp Lejeune, N.C. for at least 30 days between August 1, 1953 and December 31, 1987. Currently enrolled Veterans and new enrollees who served in a theater of combat operations after November 11, 1998, and those who were discharged from active duty on or after September 11, 2001, are eligible for the enhanced benefits for ten years post discharge.

NOTE: At the end of this 10-year enhanced enrollment period, Veterans will be assigned to the highest priority group for which their eligibility status qualifies.

Group 7: Veterans with gross household income below the geographically adjusted VA income limit for their resident location and who agree to pay copayments.

Group 8: Veterans with gross household incomes above VA's national income limit and the geographically adjusted income limit for their resident location and who agree to pay copayments.

- Veterans eligible for enrollment:

    Sub-priority a: Non-compensable 0% service-connected enrolled as of January 16, 2003, and who have remained, and who have remained enrolled since that date, and/or placed in this sub-priority due to changed eligibility status.

    Sub-priority b: Non-compensable 0% service-connected Veteran enrolled on or after June 15, 2009, whose income exceeds the current VA national income limits or VA national geographic income limits by 10% or less.

Sub-priority c: Nonservice-connected Veterans enrolled as of January 16, 2003, and who remained enrolled since that date, and/or placed in this sub-priority due to changed eligibility status.

Sub-priority d: Nonservice-connected Veterans enrolled on or after June 15, 2009, whose income exceeds the current VA national income limits or VA national geographic income limits by 10% or less.

- Veterans NOT eligible for enrollment (Veterans not meeting the criteria above):

Sub-priority e: Non-compensable 0% service-connected Veterans (eligible for care of their service-connected condition only) who are not included in sub-priority groups a or b.

Sub-priority g[1]: Nonservice-connected Veterans who are not included in sub-priority groups c or d.

VA's income limits change annually, and current levels can be found at www.va.gov/health-care/income-limits/introduction.

VA Health Care Programs and Services

VA Health Connect: VA Health Connect gets you to the right care, right now. Talk on the phone or chat online with a real person in real time 24/7 about your health care needs. With VA Health Connect, you can easily:

- Speak with a nurse about your medical or health-related questions.

- Schedule, confirm or cancel your medical appointments.

- Talk to a medical provider about an urgent or developing medical issue via phone or video.

- Refill, request medication renewals and check on the status of your medications with the help of our pharmacy professionals.

---

1   There is no Sub-priority f.

8 | Health Care

You can reach VA Health Connect by calling your local VA medical facility. If you need to find the number, check the Find VA Locations website at www.va.gov/find-locations.

You can also chat online with VA staff in most participating locations Monday to Friday, 8 a.m. to 4 p.m. local time, excluding federal holidays. In some locations, staff are available 24/7. To initiate a chat, you can access the VA Health Chat app through your internet browser or the mobile app at: mobile.va.gov/app/va-health-chat.

VA Health Connect is part of the continuity of care offered by VA. It's another way in which VA partners with you on your whole health journey. Anyone who is enrolled in health care through VA can choose telehealth visits in addition to in-person services. You may also invite a support person to join your appointment to take notes and ask questions, even if they aren't in the same location as you. After your call, the details are entered into your VA health record, so that your care team and provider can review the issue and the recommendation.

Veterans Community Care Program: Veterans may be eligible for care through a provider in their local community, depending on their health care needs or circumstances, and if they meet specific eligibility criteria. Even if eligible for community care, Veterans generally still have the option to receive care from a VA medical facility.

In most cases, Veterans must receive approval from VA before receiving care from a community provider, to avoid being billed for the care. VA staff members generally make all eligibility determinations for community care.

Eligibility: You may be eligible to see a community provider if you meet one of these six eligibility criteria:

- **Service Unavailable** – You need a service that is not available at any VA health care facility (for example, maternity care or invitro fertilization)

- **Facility Unavailable** – You reside in a U.S. state or territory without a full-service VA medical facility Specifically, this

Health Care | 9

applies to Veterans living in:

U.S. States	U.S. Territories
Alaska	Guam
Hawaii	American Samoa
New Hampshire	Northern Mariana Islands
	U.S. Virgin Islands

- **Grandfathered Choice** – You continue to reside in a location that qualified you for community care under the Veterans Choice Program's distance criteria prior to June 6, 2018, and you live in Alaska, Montana, North Dakota, South Dakota, or Wyoming.

- **Best Medical Interest** – Your VA provider determines it is in your best medical interest to be referred to a community provider.

- **Quality Standards** – You need care from a VA medical service that VA determines is not providing care that complies with VA's quality standards.

- **Access Standards** – You meet the access standards for average drive time or wait time for a VA appointment.

  A. Drive time access standards

   You may be eligible to see a community provider if your average drive time from home to a VA medical facility that provides the service you need takes more than:

   - 30 minutes travel time to receive primary care, mental health, and non-institutional extended care services (including adult home day care)

   - 60 minutes travel time to receive specialty care services

  B. Wait time access standards

   You may be eligible if the wait time for an appointment at a VA medical facility that provides the service you need exceeds:

   - 20 days for primary care, mental health, and non-institutional extended care services

10 | Health Care

- 28 days for specialty care, from the date of request, with certain exceptions

For more information, visit www.va.gov/communitycare.

Emergency Medical Care in U.S. Community Facilities

Eligible Veterans concerned that they have a medical emergency are eligible for emergency care at their nearest VA Emergency Department. Additionally, Veterans may receive emergency care at a community emergency department, possibly at VA expense, when a VA facility (or other Federal health care facility with which VA has an agreement) cannot provide timely emergency care due to the distance from the facility or when VA is unable to furnish the needed emergency services.

Since payment may be limited to the point when the condition is stable enough for the Veteran to travel to a VA facility, the community provider, Veteran or Veteran representative must contact the closest VA medical facility within 72 hours of the emergency. To notify VA, call 844-724-7842 or submit an emergency care portal notification at emergencycarereporting. communitycare.va.gov/request.

The emergency visit is deemed to have ended when a VA provider has determined that, based on sound medical judgment, the Veteran could be transferred from the community facility to a VA medical center that can accept the transfer at that time.

For more information on emergency care, visit www.va.gov/resources/getting-emergency-care-at-non-va-facilities.

Emergency Suicidal Crisis Care in U.S. Community Facilities:
If you are at imminent risk of self-harm and go to a non-VA emergency department for help, tell the staff you're a Veteran and ask them to contact us right away. Even if you are not enrolled, VA may be able to cover the cost of your emergency care and care for up to 90 days if you meet at least one of these requirements:

- You were sexually assaulted, battered, or harassed while serving in the Armed Forces, or
- You served on active duty for more than 24 months and didn't get a dishonorable discharge, or

Health Care | 11

- You served more than 100 days under a combat exclusion or in support of a contingency operation (including as a member of the Reserve) and didn't get a dishonorable discharge. You meet this requirement if you served directly or if you operated an unmanned aerial vehicle from another location.

- For immediate suicidal crisis help, including more information on eligibility and locations for care, contact the Veterans Crisis Line:

- Call: Dial 988, then Press 1

- Text: send a message to 838255

- Chat online: veteranscrisisline.net/chat

- Visit the website: veteranscrisisline.net

Urgent Care in U.S. Community Facilities:

VA provides eligible Veterans an urgent care benefit, treating injuries and illnesses that require immediate attention but are not life-threatening. This benefit includes Urgent Care treatment at local VA Urgent Cares and those in the community including diagnostic services like X-rays, some lab testing, and some medications/prescriptions (with limitations). For help with urgent care eligibility and general questions, call 1-800-MyVA411 (800-698-2411), select option 1, then select option 1 again.

When using the urgent care benefit, Veterans must go to an urgent care provider in VA's network. Upon arriving, Veterans must state they are using their VA urgent care benefit. The urgent care provider will verify the Veteran's eligibility before providing care.

For help when at the urgent care provider, call:

- 888-901-6609 if located in Region 1, 2 or 3: AL, AR, CT, DC, DE, FL, GA, IA, IL, IN, KS, KY, LA, MA, MD, ME, MI, MN, MO, MS, NC, ND, NE, NH, NJ, NY, OH, OK, PA, PR, RI, SC, SD, TN, VA, VI, VT, WI or WV

- 866-620-2071 if located in Region 4 or 5: AK, AS, AZ, CA, CO, GU, HI, ID, MP, MT, NM, NV, OR, TX, UT, WA, or WY

To find an urgent care location in VA's contracted network, Veterans can use the VA Urgent Care Locator at www.va.gov/find-locations.

Meeting the Unique Needs of Women Veterans: VA staff delivers the highest quality health care in a setting that ensures privacy, dignity, and sensitivity. Local VA facilities offer a variety of services, including women's gender-specific health, screening and disease prevention, maternity care, reproductive and routine gynecologic services, and mental health services.

Women Veterans are eligible to receive care provided in the community when they meet the eligibility criteria and are authorized by VA.

Contact a local VA facility's Women Veterans Program Manager for more information on available services, call or text 855-VA-WOMEN (855-829-6636), or visit www.womenshealth.va.gov.

VA ART/IVF Benefits under VA's Special Legislative Authority: Under Federal Law (CFR 17.380 & 17.412 FR), VA may authorize specialized fertility benefits for Veterans who have a VBA-adjudicated service-connected condition (SCC) or treatment of a SCC that results in the inability of the Veteran to procreate without the use of fertility treatments.

Assisted reproductive technologies (ART) includes all fertility treatments or procedures that include the handling of eggs alone, eggs and sperm together, or embryos for the purpose of preserving fertility or establishing a pregnancy. This includes, but is not limited to, in vitro fertilization (IVF); embryo transfer; gamete (oocyte and sperm) and embryo cryopreservation; genetic testing of the embryo(s); and manipulation of the sperm and eggs.

Veterans who are enrolled in the VA healthcare system and who have an infertility diagnosis caused by a VBA-adjudicated service-connected condition or treatment of a VBA-adjudicated SCC are eligible for VA ART/IVF benefits. These benefits are outlined in VHA Directive 1334: In Vitro Fertilization Counseling and Services Available to Certain Eligible Veterans and Their Spouses.

Eligible Veterans may be single, unmarried, or married. VA is only authorized to pay for fertility services, including IVF, for lawful spouses of eligible Veterans.

Eligible Veterans and their lawful spouse may use donor eggs, donor sperm, and donor embryos, obtained at their own expense, when receiving fertility counseling and services, including ART/IVF.

Lesbian, Gay, Bisexual, Transgender, and Queer (LGBTQ+) Veterans: LGBTQ+ Veterans are eligible for the same VA benefits as any other Veteran and will be treated in a welcoming environment. Transgender Veterans will be treated based upon their self-identified gender, including room assignments in residential and inpatient settings. There is an LGBTQ+ Veteran Care Coordinator (LGBTQ+ VCC) at every facility to help Veterans get the care they need. The LGBTQ+ VCC can answer questions, advocate for the right to quality care, handle complaints or concerns about VA care, and help Veterans get started with any VA services for LGBTQ+ Veterans.

Visit www.patientcare.va.gov/LGBT to learn more about available health care services or to find your LGBTQ+ VCC.

Same-sex couples: VA launched a website to inform Veteran and beneficiaries of the recent changes in the law and procedures involving same-sex marriages. Veterans can learn more about

VA's guidance regarding same-sex marriages at www.va.gov/opa/marriage.

Military Sexual Trauma (MST): MST is the term that VA uses to refer to sexual assault or sexual harassment occurring during military service. VA provides free treatment for physical and mental health conditions related to MST. These services are available to individuals with Veteran status and most former Service members with an Other Than Honorable or uncharacterized (entry-level) discharge. Standard length of service requirements do not apply to eligibility for MST-related care and some of these individuals may be able to receive MST-related care even if they are not eligible for other VA care. Service connection (that is, a VA disability rating) is not needed. Former National Guard and Reserves members with federal active-duty service or a service-connected disability who were discharged under honorable conditions or with an Other Than Honorable discharge can also receive MST-related care; the service-connected disability does not need to be related to their experiences of MST. To learn more about VA's MST-related services, please visit www.mentalhealth.va.gov/mst.

14 | Health Care

Mammography Screening for Veterans Exposed to Toxic Substances: All Veterans 40 and over are eligible for breast cancer screening (mammography) using guidelines from the American Cancer Society. Additionally, Veterans exposed to toxic substances (including those younger than 40) who were deployed in support of contingency operations in certain locations and during certain periods are eligible for a breast cancer risk assessment by a VA health care provider, and mammography screening as clinically appropriate.

Case Management for Transitioning Service members and Post 9/11 Era Veterans: Each VA medical center has a Post-9/11 Military2VA (M2VA) Case Management Program that provides proactive outreach, advocacy, and clinical case management services to Service members transitioning out of the military, Post-9/11 era Veterans, their caregivers, and families. Post-9/11 M2VA staff are experts in VA health care system navigation and providing a tailored and personalized approach to reintegration support. While their primary objective is to ensure transitioning Service members and Post-9/11 era Veterans are screened for early risk factors and connected to care, they stand ready to provide transition assistance to promote a successful readjustment to civilian life. More information for connecting with a local Post-9/11 M2VA team can be found at www.va.gov/POST911Veterans/index.asp.

Tax Credit: Veterans who are enrolled with VA for their health care meet the standard for minimum health care coverage; therefore, they are not eligible for assistance to lower their cost of health insurance premiums if they chose to purchase additional health insurance outside of their VA health care coverage. Veterans cannot receive a tax credit for themselves when enrolling within the marketplace, if they are currently enrolled with VA for their health care. For the latest information about VA and the health care law, visit www.va.gov/health/aca/FAQ.asp or call 877-222- VETS (877-222-8387), Monday through Friday between 8 a.m. and 8 p.m. ET, or 1-800-MyVA411 (800-698-2411), option 2.

Financial Assessment: Most Veterans not receiving VA disability compensation or pension payments must provide a financial assessment upon initial application to determine their eligibility

Health Care | 15

for free medical care, medications, and travel benefits. This financial information also may be used to determine the Veteran's enrollment priority group.

For more information, visit www.va.gov/health-care/about-va-health-benefits/cost-of-care, call toll-free 877-222-VETS (877-222-8387) Monday through Friday between 8 a.m. and 8 p.m. ET, 1-800-MyVA411 (800-698-2411), option 2, or contact the enrollment coordinator at your local VA medical facility. VA's income limits are located at www.va.gov/healthbenefits/annual_income_limits_health_benefits.asp.

- **Financial Reporting:** VA no longer requires enrolled non-service-connected and 0% non-compensable service-connected Veterans to provide their financial information annually. An assessment will continue to be collected from Veterans at the time of application for enrollment. In lieu of the annual financial reporting, VA will confirm the Veteran's financial information using information obtained from the Internal Revenue Service and Social Security Administration.

- **VA Health Care and Medication Copayments:** While many Veterans qualify for free health care based on a VA compensable service-connected condition or other special eligibilities, most Veterans are required to complete a financial assessment at the time of enrollment to determine if they qualify for free health care services. Veterans whose income exceeds the VA income limits as well as those who choose not to complete the financial assessment at the time of enrollment must agree to pay required VA copayments for care to become eligible for VA healthcare services.
  NOTE: Indian and Urban Indian Veterans are copay-exempt for all hospital care and medical services. For more information on medical services and VA copayments, visit www.va.gov/health-care/copay-rates.

- **Private Health Insurance Billing:** Veterans with private health insurance may choose to use these sources of coverage as a supplement to their VA benefits. Veterans are not responsible for paying any remaining balance of VA claims not paid or covered by their health insurance.

16 | Health Care

By law, VA is obligated to bill health insurance carriers for services provided to treat a Veteran's nonservice-connected conditions. Veterans are asked to disclose all relevant health insurance information to ensure current insurance information is on file, including coverage through a spouse.

Any payment received by VA may be used to offset a Veteran's VA copayment responsibility "dollar for dollar." Funds that VA receives from third party health insurance carriers go directly back to the VA medical center's operational budget. That money can be used to hire more staff or buy medical equipment to improve Veterans' health care. Enrolled Veterans can provide or update their insurance information by:

- Presenting their health insurance card to the VA clinic clerk
- Using a self-service kiosk at a local VA health care facility
- Using the online Health Benefits Renewal at www.va.gov/health-care/apply/application/introduction; www.va.gov/my-health/update-benefits-information-form-10-10ezr
- Calling 877-222-VETS (877-222-8387) Monday through Friday between 8 a.m. and 8 p.m. ET or 1-800-MyVA411 (800-698-2411), option 2
  - Mailing a completed paper 10-10EZR:
    - Access the following link to print a paper copy:
    - www.va.gov/find-forms/about-form-10-10ezr and mail to the:

      Health Eligibility Center
      Enrollment and Eligibility Division
      PO Box 5207
      Janesville, WI 53547-5207

VA health care is not considered health insurance. VA health care is a medical benefits package that, unless exempt, requires eligible Veterans to enroll in VA healthcare system to receive the benefits provided in the package. 38 CFR § 17.38.

Reimbursement of Travel Costs: Eligible Veterans and non-Veterans may be provided mileage reimbursement or, when medically indicated, special mode transport (for example wheelchair van, ambulance), when travel is in relation to VA medical care. Mileage reimbursement is currently 41.5 cents per mile and is a deductible of $3 one-way or $6 round-trip for each trip. The maximum deductible is $18 per calendar month.

The deductible does not apply when travel is:

- In relation to a VA compensation or pension examination; or
- By a special mode of transportation; or
- By an eligible non-Veteran; or
- When travel will cause a severe financial hardship, as defined by current regulatory guidelines.

Eligibility: A Veteran may be eligible for beneficiary travel services if one of the following criteria is met:

- Has a service-connected disability rating of 30% or more
- Is traveling for treatment of a service-connected condition
- Is traveling to obtain a service dog under 38 C.F.R. § 17.148
- Receives a VA pension, or their income does not exceed the maximum annual VA pension rate
- Is traveling for a scheduled compensation or pension examination
- Is traveling for care provided through a VA special disability rehabilitation program if the care is provided on an inpatient basis, or during a period in which the VA provides the Veteran with temporary lodging. *NOTE: This includes programs provided by spinal cord injury centers, blind rehabilitation centers, and prosthetics rehabilitee centers.*

Veterans may qualify for special mode transportation (ambulance, wheelchair van, etc.): If they meet one of the eligibility criteria in the list above and have a medical condition requiring an ambulance or a specially equipped van, as determined by a VA clinician, and the travel is preauthorized (authorization is not required for emergencies if a delay would be hazardous to life or health). More information on Beneficiary Travel is available at www.va.gov/health-care/get-reimbursed-for-travel-pay.

18 | Health Care

Veteran Health Registries: Certain Veterans can participate in a VA health registry and receive free environmental health evaluations and related information. To participate, contact the environmental health coordinator at your nearest VA health care facility or call 1-800-MyVA411 (800-698-2411), option 8. You can find an environmental coordinator near you by visiting www.publichealth.va.gov/exposures/coordinators.asp.

Veterans should be aware that a health registry evaluation is not a disability compensation exam. A registry evaluation does not start a claim for compensation and is not required for any VA benefits. To learn more, and for a list of current health registries, visit www.publichealth.va.gov/exposures/benefits/registry-evaluation.asp.

Electronic Health Information Sharing Options: VA believes providers can make more informed treatment decisions, which drive better health outcomes, when they have a complete view of a patient's medical history. VA electronically shares health information using one of the health information exchange tools. Electronic health information may be shared with participating non-VA partners/providers who are part of a VA Patient's health care team in order to provide continued care coordination. Seamless and secure sharing using electronic health information exchange means your health care team is able to better understand your health history and coordinate your care for better outcomes.

The notice on how VA uses and shares electronic health care information is available at www.va.gov/VHIE under Privacy and HIE, Notice of Privacy Practices and at www.va.gov/resources/about-electronic-health-information-sharing-at-va.

Want to opt out of sharing your electronic health information?

You can opt out by choosing one of the following options:

- Online: Sign in to the My HealtheVet website with your Login.gov or ID.me account. Go to Health Records and select Electronic Sharing Options. Then select Opt Out.

- By Mail: Download and print *VA Form 10-10164, Opt-Out of Sharing Protected Health Information Through Health Information Exchanges*

- Mail the completed form to your local VAMC, attention Release of Information Office
- In Person: Visit the ROI Office at your local VAMC

If you opt out but want to resume secure, seamless sharing, you may do so at any time by completing *VA Form 10-10163, Request For and Permission to Participate in Sharing Protected Health Information Through Health Information Exchanges*, then mail to or visit the ROI Office at your local VAMC. Online: Sign in to the My HeatheVet website with your Login.gov or ID.me account. Go to Health Records and select Electronic Sharing Options. Then select Opt Back In.

Vet Center Services: (www.vetcenter.va.gov) Vet Centers provide confidential, community- based counseling, outreach, and referral services for a wide range of concerns that eligible Veterans, Service members, including members of the National Guard and Reserve Components and their families may face. Vet Centers help you and your family build meaningful connections and develop tools for achieving success in both your military and civilian lives. In addition to referral and connection to other VA and community benefits and services, individual, group, marriage, and family counseling are offered at no cost and without time limitation.

If you are a Veteran or Service member, including members of the National Guard and Reserve, you can access our services if you:

- Served on active military duty in any combat theater or area of hostility
- Experienced MST (regardless of gender or service era)
- Provided mortuary services or direct emergent medical care to treat the casualties of war while serving on active military duty
- Performed as a member of an unmanned aerial vehicle crew that provided direct support to operations in a combat theater or area of hostility
- Accessed care at a Vet Center prior to January 2, 2013, as a Vietnam-Era Veteran
- Served on active military duty in response to a national emergency or major disaster declared by the president, or

20 | Health Care

under orders of the governor or chief executive of a state in response to a disaster or civil disorder in that state

- Are a current or former member of the Coast Guard who participated in a drug interdiction operation, regardless of the location

- Are a current member of the reserve components assigned to a military command in a drilling status, including active Reserves, who has a behavioral health condition or psychological trauma related to military service that adversely effects quality of life or adjustment to civilian life

- Are a Veteran or service member pursuing a course of education using covered educational assistance benefits and have a readjustment counseling need that is related to the individual's military service and hinders the individual's adjustment to either their civilian life, ongoing military service, or educational settings

Vet Center services are also available to family members when their participation would support the growth and goals of the Veteran or Service member. Vet Centers offer confidential, no-cost bereavement counseling services to family members of: 1. Armed Forces personnel who died in the service of our country; 2. Reservists and National Guardsmen who die while on duty; 3. Veteran who was receiving Vet Center services at the time of the Veteran's death if the death was unexpected or occurred while the eligible individual was receiving hospice or similar care; 4. Veterans and service members who die by suicide to assist them in coping with the effects of suicide. This bereavement counseling is provided at community-based Vet Centers located near the families.

To connect with local services, contact the Vet Center Call Center 24/7 by dialing 1-877-927-8387 or use the Location Finder (www.va.gov/find-locations) to find the nearest Vet Center, 24/7 at 877-927-8387.

Home Improvements and Structural Alterations: VA provides up to $6,800 in lifetime benefits for service-connected Veterans and up to $2,000 in lifetime benefits for non-service-connected Veterans to make home improvements and/or structural changes necessary for the continuation of treatment or for disability access to the Veterans home and essential lavatory and sanitary facilities. For application information, contact the prosthetic representative at the nearest VA medical center.

Spina Bifida Health Care Benefits Program (SBHCBP): For certain Korea, Vietnam, and Thailand Veterans' birth children diagnosed with spina bifida (except spina bifida occulta), VA provides comprehensive health care benefits, including outpatient, inpatient, pharmacy, prosthetics, medical equipment, and supplies. For more information, visit www.va.gov/COMMUNITYCARE/programs/dependents/spinabifida.

Services for Blind and Visually Impaired Veterans: Veterans with visual impairments may be eligible for lifetime care coordination at a VA medical center and for services provided by an inpatient or outpatient VA blind and vision rehabilitation program.

Mental Health Care Treatment: Veterans eligible for VA medical care may receive general and specialty mental health treatment as needed, including individual, group, and family therapy options. Mental health services are available in primary care clinics (including Home Based Primary Care), general and specialty mental health outpatient clinics, residential rehabilitation treatment programs, inpatient mental health units, specialty medical clinics, and Community Living Centers. Veterans have multiple options for their care delivery, including telehealth and in-person care. For more information on VA mental health services:

- Visit www.va.gov/health-care/health-needs-conditions/mental-health
- Visit www.mentalhealth.va.gov
- Contact your local VA health care facility's Enrollment Office

Veterans Crisis Line: The Veterans Crisis Line connects Veterans, Service Members, and concerned parties in crisis, and their families and friends, with qualified, caring VA responders through a confidential toll-free hotline, text messaging service, or online chat. Veterans and their loved ones can:

- Dial 988 then Press 1
- Send a text message to 838255, or
- Chat online at VeteransCrisisLine.net/chat

22 | Health Care

The professionals at the Veterans Crisis Line are specially trained and experienced in helping Veterans, service members, and concerned parties of all ages and circumstances. VA offers a network of support for all Veterans, their families, and friends. You don't have to be enrolled in VA benefits or health care to connect.

Veterans, service members, as well as members of the National Guard and Reserve, outside of the continental U.S. (OCONUS) can visit VeteransCrisisLine.net to find contact information by region or to chat online with responders.

For more information about VA's suicide prevention program, visit www.mentalhealth.va.gov/suicide_prevention.

VA Dental Insurance Program: VA would like all Veterans to have access to good oral health care; however, VA is limited to providing dental benefits to those Veterans who meet certain eligibility criteria. To help Veterans who are not eligible for VA dental benefits or need more comprehensive dental care, VA offers enrolled Veterans and beneficiaries of CHAMPVA the opportunity to purchase dental insurance at a reduced cost through its VA Dental Insurance Program (VADIP).

Delta Dental of California and MetLife offer private dental insurance plans for enrolled Veterans and beneficiaries of CHAMPVA for VADIP. VADIP provides eligible individuals the opportunity to purchase discounted dental insurance coverage, including diagnostic services, preventive services, endodontic and other restorative services, surgical services, and emergency services. Individuals who enroll in one of the dental insurance plans are responsible for paying the entire premium in addition to the full cost of any copayments. Enrollment is voluntary and does not affect eligibility for VA outpatient dental services and treatment. The plans are available to eligible individuals in the U.S., the District of Columbia, Puerto Rico, Guam, the U.S. Virgin Islands, American Samoa, and the Commonwealth of the Northern Mariana Islands.

For more information about this program, call toll-free 877- 222- VETS (8387) Monday through Friday between 8 a.m. and 8 p.m. ET, or visit www.va.gov/healthbenefits/vadip. Veterans and CHAMPVA

Health Care | 23

beneficiaries may also review each insurer for specific information regarding their registration, rates, and services: Delta Dental at www.deltadentalins.com/vadip or call 855-370-3303; MetLife at www.metlife.com/VADIP or call 888-310-1681.

Long-term Services and Supports: VA provides a spectrum of home and community-based long-term services to Veterans, ranging from primary care at home-to-home health aide and in- home respite services. Each program has admission and eligibility criteria specific to the program. VA also provides facility-based services (nursing home level of care) to Veterans through three national programs: VA-owned and operated Community Living Centers, State Veterans Homes owned and operated by the states, and the community nursing home program. Each program has admission and eligibility criteria specific to the program. VA is obligated to pay the full cost of nursing home services for enrolled Veterans who need nursing home care for a service-connected disability or Veterans who have a 70% or greater service-connected disability and Veterans with a rating of total disability based on individual unemployability. VA-provided nursing home care for all other Veterans is based on available resources. For more information on extended care services and geriatrics visit www.va.gov/GERIATRICS/index.asp.

State Home Per Diem Program: The Veterans Health Administration (VHA) State Home Per Diem Program is a grant program providing federal assistance to Veterans receiving care in VA-recognized State Veterans Homes (SVH) facilities. Additionally, VHA pays a daily payment to the qualifying SVHs for nursing home, domiciliary, or adult day health care provided to eligible Veterans. For additional information please visit www.va.gov/geriatrics/pages/State_Veterans_Home_Program_Topics.asp or email VHA12GECStateHomePerDiemInquiries@va.gov.

Foreign Medical Program: VA's Foreign Medical Program (FMP) pays/reimburses healthcare claims for the treatment of the U.S. Veteran's VA-rated service-connected disability, or any disability associated with and held to be aggravating a service-connected disability, while the Veteran is living or traveling abroad.

All Veterans living or planning to travel outside the U.S. should

24 | Health Care

register with FMP. *VA Form 10-7959f-1* can be downloaded at www.va.gov/find-forms/about-form-10-7959f-1. The completed form may be submitted by faxing to 303-331-7803, or by mailing to:

VHA Office of Integrated Veteran Care
Foreign Medical Program (FMP)
PO Box 469061
Denver, CO 80246-9061
USA

For more information, including ways to contact FMP staff and how to file FMP medical claims, call 303-331-7590 (TTY: 711) or visit www.va.gov/health-care/foreign-medical-program.

Traveling Veterans: Enrolled Veterans who receive their health care with VA will receive the same coordinated care, whether at their local VA treatment site or an alternate VA site of care. To help VA ensure Veterans receive consistent care while they are traveling, Veterans are asked to notify their VA Patient Aligned Care Team (PACT) and specialty care provider(s) four to six weeks before traveling, or as soon as possible. Early planning will allow time for PACT and the Traveling Veteran Coordinator to coordinate care at an alternate VA facility. VA providers at the alternate site will record the care in the Veteran's electronic medical record for follow-up treatment options with their PACT. To coordinate health care with another VA health care facility, Veterans should inform their PACT of the following:

- Travel destination(s) and temporary address
- Valid telephone number
- Arrival and departure dates
- Specific care concerns

Their PACT will contact the Traveling Veteran Coordinator, who will assist in coordinating care at the alternate facility. For more information, contact PACT or a Traveling Veteran Coordinator at the local VA facility.

Veteran Health Identification Card: To get a Veteran ID Card go to www.va.gov/records/get-veteran-id-cards/vic. When you're enrolled in VA health care, you'll use your Veteran Health

Identification Card (VHIC) to check in to your appointments at VA medical centers. This secure ID card keeps your personal information safe while giving us the information we need to easily access your VA health record.

Caregiver Support Program and Services: Caregivers are eligible for a host of VA services offered through VA's Program of General Caregiver Support Services (PGCSS) and Program of Comprehensive Assistance for Family Caregivers (PCAFC) collectively known as the Caregiver Support Program (CSP). PGCSS provides services and supports to caregivers of Veterans enrolled in and receiving health care at any Veterans Health Administration facility.

PGCSS offers peer support mentoring, training, education, respite care, self-care courses, referrals, and the Caregiver Support Line 855-260-3274. In addition to services offered under the PGCSS, VA offers enhanced clinical support for Family Caregivers of eligible Veterans through PCAFC. Eligible Primary Family Caregivers enrolled in PCAFC may also receive a monthly stipend, beneficiary travel, mental health counseling, enhanced respite services and health insurance, if applicable. To learn more about eligibility and the application process for PCAFC, visit www.caregiver.va.gov/support/support_benefits.asp.

For detailed information about VA's Caregiver Support Program (CSP) and the full range of services available to caregivers, visit www.caregiver.va.gov.

Dependents and Survivors Health Care - Civilian Health and Medical Program of the Department of Veterans Affairs (CHAMPVA): Under CHAMPVA, certain dependents and survivors can receive reimbursement for most medical expenses – such as inpatient, outpatient, mental health, prescription medication, skilled nursing care and durable medical equipment.

To be eligible for CHAMPVA a Veteran's spouse or surviving spouse and eligible family members must not be eligible for TRICARE, which is the medical program provided for civilian dependents through the Department of Defense (DoD). The Veteran must also meet one of the following criteria:

26 | Health Care

- Rated permanently and totally (P&T) disabled for a service-connected disability by a VA regional office (VARO), without regard to percentage of disability
- Died from a VA-rated service-connected disability
- At the time of death was rated P&T disabled from a service-connected disability
- Died in the line of duty, not due to misconduct; however, most of these family members qualify for TRICARE instead of CHAMPVA

A surviving spouse under age 55 who remarries loses CHAMPVA eligibility at midnight on the date of remarriage. The surviving spouse may re-establish eligibility if the remarriage ends by death, divorce, or annulment effective the first day of the month following the termination of the remarriage or December 1, 1999, whichever is later. A surviving spouse who remarries after age 55 does not lose eligibility upon remarriage.

CHAMPVA is a secondary payer whenever a beneficiary has other health insurance (OHI), to include Medicare. Beneficiaries who are eligible for Medicare must maintain continuous enrollment in Medicare Part B to retain CHAMPVA eligibility.

For more information about CHAMPVA, including how to apply, please call 800-733-8387 or visit www.va.gov/communitycare/programs/dependents/champva.

CHAMPVA benefits may also be available to the Primary Family Caregiver of a Veteran if the caregiver does not have OHI. For more information, visit www.caregiver.va.gov.

Camp Lejeune Family Member Program: The Camp Lejeune Family Member Program (CLFMP) is a medical care cost reimbursement program for family members of Veterans who were stationed at Camp Lejeune between August 1, 1953, through December 31, 1987. VA will reimburse eligible Camp Lejeune Family Members for health care costs related to one or more of 15 specified illnesses or medical conditions. For more information visit www.clfamilymembers.fsc.va.gov or call the toll-free CLFMP customer service line at 866-372-1144.

Non-Health Care Benefits

Disabled Veterans

Disability Compensation: Disability compensation is a tax-free monetary benefit, paid to Veterans with disabilities that are the result of a disease or injury incurred or aggravated during active military service, to include physical and mental health conditions resulting from MST. The benefits amount is graduated according to the degree of the Veteran's disability on a scale from 10% to 100% (in increments of 10%). Compensation may also be paid for disabilities that are considered related or secondary to disabilities incurred in service, even though they may arise after service.

To be eligible for compensation, a Veteran must have been separated or discharged under conditions other than dishonorable. For more information on eligibility for VA disability benefits, visit www.va.gov/disability/eligibility.

Monthly disability compensation rates vary based on the degree of disability and the number of eligible dependents. Veterans with disability ratings of at least 30% are eligible for additional allowances for dependents, including spouses, minor children, children between the ages of 18 and 23 who are attending school, children who are permanently incapable of self-support because of a disability arising before age 18, and dependent parents.

The additional amount depends on the disability rating and the number of dependents. For detailed compensation rate information visit www.va.gov/disability/compensation-rates/veteran-rates.

The Benefits Delivery at Discharge (BDD) Program allows transitioning Service members to apply for their disability benefits prior to separation. This provides time for VA to schedule exams, review service treatment records, and evaluate the claim before separation, thus allowing Veterans the opportunity to receive benefits sooner. Some BDD claimants receive their decision as soon as the day after leaving active duty. For more information on VA's Pre-Discharge Programs visit www.va.gov/disability/how-to-file-claim/when-to-file/pre-discharge-claim.

28 | Non-Health Care Benefits

Military retirement pay, disability severance pay, separation incentive pay (Special Separation Benefit), Reservists' Involuntary Separation Pay, and Voluntary Separation Pay may affect the amount of VA compensation paid to disabled Veterans. For additional details on types of disability claims and how to apply, visit www.benefits.va.gov/compensation.

Special Monthly Compensation (SMC): SMC is an additional tax-free benefit that can be paid to Veterans. For Veterans, SMC is a higher rate of compensation paid, due to special circumstances such as the need for aid and attendance by another person, or due to a specific disability such as the loss of use of one hand, leg or reproductive organ. A Veteran who is determined by VA to need the regular aid and attendance of another person or a Veteran who is permanently housebound may be entitled to additional payments. For detailed special monthly compensation rate information visit www.va.gov/disability/compensation-rates/special-monthly-compensation-rates.

Adoption Expenses Reimbursement: Covered Veterans may request reimbursement up to $2,000 per adopted child for qualifying adoption expenses incurred by the Veteran in the adoption of a child under 18 years of age. An adoption for which expenses may be reimbursed includes an adoption by a married or single person, an infant adoption, an intercountry adoption, and an adoption of a child with special needs (as defined in section 473 of the Social Security Act (42 U.S.C. 673(c)).

Reimbursement for qualifying adoption expenses may be requested only for an adoption that became final after September 29, 2016. In the case of adoption of a foreign child, reimbursement for qualifying adoption expenses may be requested only after United States citizenship has been granted to the adopted child.

Reimbursement for qualifying adoption expenses may not be paid for expense paid to or for a covered Veteran under any other adoption benefits program administered by the Federal Government or under any such program administered by a State or local government.

Who is a covered Veteran? "Covered Veteran" means a Veteran with a service-connected disability that results in the inability of the Veteran to procreate without the use of fertility treatment.

"Service-connected disability that results in the inability of the Veteran to procreate without the use of fertility" means for a male Veteran, a service-connected injury or illness that prevents the successful delivery of sperm to an egg; and, for a female Veteran with ovarian function and a patent uterine cavity, a service-connected injury or illness that prevents the egg from being successfully fertilized by sperm.

Automobile Allowance: Beginning October 1, 2023, Service members and Veterans may be eligible for a payment of $25,603.02, toward the purchase of an automobile or other conveyance if they have certain service-connected disabilities. Effective January 5, 2023, VA may provide or assist in providing an additional automobile or other conveyance if more than 30 years have passed since the Veteran or Service member most recently received VA financial assistance to purchase an automobile or other conveyance.

Rates can be found at www.va.gov/disability/compensation-rates/special-benefit-allowance-rates.

To apply, contact a VA regional office at 800-827-1000, 1-800-MyVA411 (800-698-2411), option 5, or the nearest VA health care facility, which can be found using VA's facility locator: www.va.gov/directory/guide/home.asp. An application for benefits may also be made online at www.va.gov.

Clothing Allowance: Any Veteran who has service-connected disabilities that require prosthetic or orthopedic appliances may receive clothing allowances. The prescribed device must cause wear and tear to the clothing. This allowance is also available to any Veteran whose service-connected skin condition requires prescribed skin medication that irreparably damages their outer garments. To receive an entitlement decision, an application must be received by August 1st of the benefit year you are claiming. To apply for a recurring / continuous annual payment, contact the prosthetic representative at the nearest VA medical center located at www.va.gov/find-locations. For information on current rates visit www.va.gov/disability/compensation-rates/special-benefit-allowance-rates.

Additional Benefits for Eligible Military Retirees: Concurrent Retirement and Disability Pay (CRDP) is a program that allows some individuals to receive both military retired pay and VA disability compensation simultaneously. Normally, such concurrent receipt is prohibited. Veterans do not need to apply for this benefit, as payment is coordinated between VA and the military pay center. To qualify for CRDP, Veterans must have a VA service-connected disability rating of 50% or greater, be eligible to receive retired pay and:

- Must have retired from military service based on longevity, including Temporary Early Retirement Authority retirees; or
- Must have retired due to disability with 20 or more years of service*; or
- Must have retired from National Guard or Reserve service with 20 or more qualifying years.

*For Veterans who retired due to disability with 20 or more years of service, CRDP is subject to an offset for the difference between retired pay based on disability and retired pay based on longevity.

Housing Grants for Disabled Veterans: Service members and Veterans with certain service-connected disabilities may be entitled to a housing grant from VA to help build a new specially adapted house, to adapt a home they already own, or buy a house and modify it to meet their disability-related requirements.

Eligible Veterans or Service members may now receive up to six uses of the grant, with the total dollar amount of the grants not to exceed the maximum allowable amount. Housing grant amounts may be adjusted October 1 every year based on a cost-of-construction index. These adjustments will increase the grant amounts or leave them unchanged; grant amounts will not decrease. Previous grant recipients who had received assistance of less than the current maximum allowable may be eligible for an additional grant. To obtain general information about the Specially Adapted Housing program, visit www.va.gov/housing-assistance/

Non-Health Care Benefits | 31

disability-housing-grants or call the program's local office of jurisdiction at 877-827-3702 or 1-800-MyVA411 (800-698-2411), option 5.

Specially Adapted Housing (SAH) Grant: VA may approve a grant to assist with the cost of building, buying, adapting existing homes or paying to reduce indebtedness on a currently owned home that is being adapted, up to a maximum benefit amount.

Rates can be found by visiting www.va.gov/housing-assistance/disability-housing-grants. The SAH grant is available to certain Veterans and Service members who are entitled to disability compensation due to the following:

- The loss, or loss of use, of more than one limb

- The loss, or loss of use, of a lower extremity along with the residuals (lasting effects) of an organic (natural) disease or injury

- Blindness in both eyes (with 20/200 central visual acuity or less)

- Certain severe burns

- The loss, or loss of use, of one lower extremity (foot or leg) after September 11, 2001, which makes it so that you cannot balance or walk without the help of braces, crutches, canes, or a wheelchair.

- Both of these must be true:
  - You own or will own the home, and
  - You have a qualifying service-connected disability

NOTE: The property may be located outside the U.S., in a country or political subdivision which allows individuals to have or acquire a beneficial property interest and in which the Secretary of Veteran Affairs, in his or her discretion, has determined that is reasonably practicable to aid in acquiring specially adapted housing. For more information on SAH, visit www.va.gov/housing-assistance/disability-housing-grants or call the program's local office of jurisdiction at 877-827-3702.

*Receiving a grant may also provide access to Veterans Mortgage

Life Insurance (VMLI), Veterans' Mortgage Life Insurance (VMLI) | Veterans Affairs (www.va.gov).

Special Home Adaptation (SHA) Grant: VA may approve a grant to assist with the cost of adapting or purchasing a home to live more independently. Service member Information on current rates may be found by visiting www.va.gov/housing-assistance/disability-housing-grants. To be eligible for this grant, Service members and Veterans must be entitled to compensation for permanent and total service-connected disability due to one of the following:

- Anatomical loss or loss of use of both hands
- Certain severe burn injuries
- Certain severe respiratory injuries

*Receiving a grant may also provide access to VMLI.

Temporary Residence Adaptation (TRA): Eligible Veterans and Service members who are temporarily residing in a home owned by a family member may also receive a TRA grant to adapt the family member's home to meet his or her specific needs. Information on current rates may be found by visiting: www.va.gov/housing-assistance/disability-housing-grants.

NOTE: TRA grant amounts do not count against SAH or SHA grant maximum amounts.

Supplemental Financing: Veterans and Service members with available VA Home Loan Guaranty entitlement may also obtain a guaranteed loan to supplement the grant to acquire a specially adapted home that has already been adapted. For more information on SAH, visit www.va.gov/housing-assistance/disability-housing-grants.

Veteran Readiness and Employment

Veteran Readiness and Employment (VR&E): VR&E, also referred to as the Chapter 31 program, provides services to eligible Service members and Veterans with service-connected disabilities and an employment handicap to help them to prepare for, obtain, and maintain suitable employment. For Veterans and Service members with service-connected disabilities so severe that they cannot immediately consider work, VR&E provides services to improve their ability to live as independently as possible. For additional information on VR&E benefits please visit www.va.gov/vre.

VR&E Eligibility for Veterans: A Veteran must have a VA service-connected disability rating of at least 20% and determined to have an employment handicap, or rated 10% and determined to have a serious employment handicap, and must be discharged or released from active military service under other than dishonorable conditions.

VR&E Eligibility for Service members: Service members are eligible to apply if they expect to receive an honorable discharge upon separation from active duty; and obtain a memorandum rating of 20% or more from VA, or automatic entitlement through the Integrated Disability Evaluation System.

VR&E Entitlement: A Vocational Rehabilitation Counselor (VRC) works with the Veteran to determine if an employment handicap exists. An employment handicap exists if a Veteran's service-connected disability impairs his/her ability to prepare for, obtain, and maintain suitable employment. After a favorable entitlement decision is made, the Veteran and VRC work together to develop an individualized rehabilitation plan.

VR&E Services: Veterans work with a VRC to select one of the five tracks to employment based on their individual needs.

If a program of training is selected, VA pays the cost of the approved training and services that are outlined in the Veteran's rehabilitation plan (except those coordinated through other providers), as well as a subsistence allowance.

The Five Tracks to Employment are:

- <u>Reemployment</u> targets Veterans and Service members who served on active military service or in the National Guard or Reserves and now returning to employers for whom they worked prior to going on active duty. Reemployment is protected under Uniformed Services Employment and Reemployment Rights Act (USERRA).

- <u>Rapid access to employment</u> targets Veterans who express a desire to obtain employment as soon as possible and already have the necessary skills to qualify for competitive employment in a suitable job.

- <u>Self-employment</u> targets Veterans who have limited access to traditional employment, need flexible work schedules, or need a more accommodating work environment due to their disabling conditions or other life circumstances.

- <u>Employment through long-term services</u> targets Veterans who need long-term services such as remedial or refresher courses, specialized training and/or post-secondary education, to obtain and/or maintain suitable employment.

- <u>Independent living</u> targets Veterans who may be unable to immediately return to work, but with assistance of VR&E services, they are able to improve their independence in daily living.

Period of a Rehabilitation Program: The basic period of eligibility in which VR&E benefits may be used is 12 years from 1) A Veteran's date of separation from active military service or 2) the date VA first notified a Veteran that they have been granted a compensable service-connected disability, whichever is later. As of January 5, 2021, the 12-year eligibility period does not apply to claimants who were discharged or released from active military service on or after January 1, 2013. Veterans may be provided up to 48 months of full-time services or the part-time equivalent based on the extent of services needed to complete the rehabilitation program. Rehabilitation plans that provide services to achieve the maximum level of independence cannot exceed 24 months but may be extended in certain circumstances.

VR&E 2101B Housing Adaptation Grant: VR&E may provide home adaptations to Veterans and Service members who are not currently able to work because of the effects of their service-connected disabilities or who require adaptations to achieve a vocational goal. The benefits are limited to those required to improve independence at home and/or in the community.

Home adaptations may be provided as part of an approved rehabilitation plan. The maximum amounts may change from year-to-year and are located www.va.gov/housing-assistance/disability-housing-grants. For more information about Independent Living, visit www.va.gov/careers-employment/vocational-rehabilitation/programs/independent-living.

Employment Services: In partnership with the U.S. Department of Labor, VA provides support to Veterans and transitioning Service members at all stages of their job search, including career advice, resume building, and access to employers who want to hire Veterans and military spouses. Additional information and access to services are available at www.va.gov/careers-employment.

VR&E also establishes partnerships with Federal, state, and private agencies that help facilitate direct placement of Veterans or Service members into civilian careers. VR&E can assist with placement using the following resources:

- **On the Job Training (OJT) Program:** Employers hire Veterans at an apprentice wage and VR&E supplements the salary at the journeyman wage (up to the maximum amount allowable under OJT). As the Veterans progress through training, the employers begin to increase the salary until the Veterans reach journeyperson level and the employers pay the entire salary. VR&E may also pay for any necessary tools.

- **Non-Paid Work Experience (NPWE):** The NPWE program provides eligible Veterans the opportunity to obtain training and practical job experience concurrently. This program is ideal for Veterans or Service members who have a clearly established vocational goal and who learn easily in a hands-on environment. This program is also well suited forVeterans who are having difficulties obtaining employment due to lack

36 | Veteran Readiness and Employment

of work experience.

The NPWE program may be established in a federal, state, or local (such as a county, city, town, or school district) government agency only. The employer may hire the Veteran at any point during the NPWE program.

- **Special Employer Incentive (SEI):** The SEI program is for eligible Veterans who face challenges in obtaining employment. Veterans approved to participate in the SEI program are hired by participating employers and employment is expected to continue following successful completion of the program. Employers are provided this incentive to hire Veterans. If approved, the employer will receive reimbursement for up to 50% of the Veteran's salary during the SEI program, which can last up to six months.

- **VetSuccess on Campus (VSOC):** The VSOC program aims to help Veterans, Service members, and eligible dependents succeed through a coordinated delivery of on-campus benefits assistance and counseling, leading to successful completion of their education and preparing them to enter the labor market in viable careers. For additional information on the VSOC program please visit www.benefits.va.gov/vocrehab/vsoc.asp.

- **Chapter 36 Personalized Career Planning and Guidance:** VA's Education and Career Counseling Program (Title 38 U.S.C. Chapter 36) offers a great opportunity for transitioning Veterans, Service members, and dependents to get personalized counseling and support to guide their career paths and help them achieve their goals. For additional information please visit www.va.gov/careers-employment/education-and-career-counseling.

Pension

VA Pension: VA helps Veterans, and their families cope with financial challenges by providing supplemental income through the Veterans Pension and Survivors Pension benefit programs. Payments are made to bring the Veteran's or survivor's total income, including other retirement or Social Security income, to a level set by Congress. Unreimbursed medical expenses may reduce countable income for VA purposes.

Veterans Pension: Congress establishes the maximum annual pension rate. Payments are reduced by the amount of countable income of the Veteran, spouse, and dependent children. When a Veteran without a dependent is furnished nursing home or domiciliary care by VA, the pension is reduced to an amount not to exceed $90 per month after three calendar months of care. The reduction may be delayed if nursing home care continues to provide the Veteran with rehabilitation services. For additional information on pension benefits please visit www.va.gov/pension.

Eligibility for Veterans Pension: Veterans who entered active duty after September 7, 1980, generally must have served at least 24 months or for the full period for which they called or ordered to active duty (with some exceptions), with at least one day during a wartime period. For those separated prior to September 7, 1980, a Veteran must have at least 90 days of active military service, with at least one day during a recognized wartime period to qualify for a VA pension. The 90-day active military service requirement does not apply to Veterans discharged from the military due to a service-connected disability. The Veteran's discharge must have been under conditions other than dishonorable, and the disability must be for reasons other than the Veteran's own willful misconduct. In addition to meeting the minimum service requirement, low-income wartime Veterans may qualify for pension if they meet certain service, income, and net worth limits set by law and are:

- Age 65 or older; or
- Permanently and totally disabled; or
- A patient in a nursing home receiving skilled nursing care; or

38 | Pension

- VA-approved medical foster home; or
- Receiving Social Security Disability Insurance; or
- Receiving Supplemental Security Income.

Yearly family income and net worth must be less than the amount set by Congress to qualify for the Veterans pension benefit. Payments are made to bring the Veteran's total income, including other retirement or Social Security income, to a level set by Congress. Unreimbursed medical expenses may reduce countable income for VA purposes.

How to Apply for Veterans Pension: To apply for Veterans Pension, download and complete *VA Form 21P 527EZ, "Application for Veterans Pension."* You can mail your application to the address below:

Department of Veterans Affairs
Pension Intake Center
P.O. Box 5365
Janesville, WI 53547

Aid and Attendance and Housebound Benefits (Special Monthly Pension): Veterans who are eligible for VA pension and require the aid and attendance of another person, or are housebound, may be eligible for a higher maximum annual pension rate. These benefits are paid in addition to monthly pension, and they are not paid without eligibility for pension. Since aid and attendance and housebound allowances increase the pension amount, people who are not eligible for a basic pension due to excessive income may be eligible for pension at these increased rates. A Veteran may not receive aid and attendance benefits and housebound benefits at the same time. For additional information on aid and attendance and housebound benefits including how to apply please visit www.va.gov/pension/aid-attendance-housebound.

To apply for aid and attendance or housebound benefits, submit a *VA Form 21-2680, Examination for Housebound Status or Permanent Need for Regular Aid and Attendance,* to the following address:

Pension | 39

U.S. Department of Veterans Affairs
Pension Intake Center
P.O. Box 5365
Janesville, WI 53547

Please include copies of any evidence, preferably a report from an attending physician or a nursing home, validating the need for aid and attendance or housebound status. The report should contain enough detail to determine whether there is disease or injury producing physical or mental impairment, loss of coordination, or conditions affecting the ability to dress and undress, to feed oneself, to attend to sanitary needs and to keep oneself ordinarily clean and presentable, or whether confined to the immediate premises due to disability.

Reductions for Medicaid Covered Nursing Facility Care:
Veterans with no dependents who are in a Medicaid-approved nursing facility and covered by a Medicaid plan for services furnished by the nursing facility are limited to receiving $90 per month in pension benefits. No part of the $90 monthly pension may be used to reduce the amount of Medicaid paid to a nursing facility.

Education and Training

Education and Training Benefits help Veterans, Service members and their qualified family members with needs like paying college tuition, finding the right school, or training program, and getting career counseling.

Post–9/11 GI Bill: The Post-9/11 GI Bill is an education benefit program for Service members and Veterans who served on active duty after September 10, 2001. For additional information on education and training opportunities please visit www.va.gov/education/about-gi-bill-benefits/post-9-11 or call 888-GI-BILL-1 (888-442-4551) or 1-800-MyVA411 (800-698-2411), option 5.

Post–9/11 GI Bill Eligibility: To be eligible, the Service member or Veteran must serve at least 90 aggregate days on active duty after September 10, 2001, and remain on active duty or be honorably discharged. Active duty includes active service performed by National Guard members under title 32 U.S.C. for the purposes of organizing, administering, recruiting, instructing, or training the National Guard; or under section 502(f) for the purpose of responding to a national emergency. Veterans may also be eligible if they were honorably discharged from active duty for a service-connected disability after serving 30 continuous days after September 10, 2001. Additionally, under the Colmery Act of 2017, all Purple Heart award recipients are eligible for Post-9/11 GI Bill entitlement providing the award was made during service occurring after September 10, 2001 and the recipient continued duty or received an honorable discharge.

Contents of Benefit: Generally, Service members or eligible Veterans may receive up to 36 months of entitlement under the Post-9/11 GI Bill. No beneficiary may use more than 48 months of education and training benefits from any combination of programs, with the exception of VR&E benefits. Approved training under the Post-9/11 GI Bill includes graduate and undergraduate degrees, vocational/technical training, on-the-job and apprenticeship training, flight training, correspondence training, licensing and national testing programs, and tutorial assistance.

Based on the length of active-duty service, eligible participants are entitled to receive a percentage of the cost of in-state tuition and fees at public institutions, or the tuition and fees capped at a national maximum rate for private or foreign schools. Current rates can be found at www.va.gov/education/benefit-rates.

If a Service member or Veteran is eligible for the Montgomery GI Bill or the Montgomery GI Bill-Selected Reserve and qualifies for the Post-9/11 GI Bill, an irrevocable election must be made to receive benefits under the Post-9/11 GI Bill. That means in most instances, once the election to receive benefits under the Post-9/11 GI Bill is made, the individual will no longer be eligible to receive benefits under the relinquished program.

Tuition and fees are paid to the institution on the student's behalf. As well, a monthly housing allowance (MHA) is paid directly to the student, provided the student is attending more than half time. Currently, MHA is equal to the basic allowance for housing payable to a military E-5 with dependents but prorated based on benefit level and rate of pursuit (e.g., full- time student, ¾-time student, etc.). MHA is calculated based on the ZIP code of the campus location where the student physically attends most of their classes. If a student is only taking online courses, their MHA is half the national average. Please note, however, that MHA is not payable to individuals enrolled in flight or correspondence training; to individuals while pursuing training at half time or less (regardless of the type of training); or to individuals while on active duty or their spouses. Current rates can be found at www.va.gov/education/benefit-rates. Additional benefits under the Post-9/11 GI Bill include a yearly books and supplies stipend of up to $1,000 per year (paid directly to the Service member, Veteran, or eligible dependents) and a one-time payment of $500 paid to certain individuals relocating from highly rural areas.

The Yellow Ribbon G.I. Bill Education Enhancement Program:
The Yellow Ribbon Program allows institutions of higher learning (such as colleges, universities, and other degree-granting schools) in the U.S. and overseas to voluntarily enter into an agreement with VA to fund tuition and fees that exceed theamounts payable under the Post-9/11 GI Bill. The institution can contribute a

42 | Education and Training

specified dollar amount of those expenses and VA will match the contribution not to exceed 50% of the difference. To be eligible, the student must be a Veteran, active-duty Service member, individual awarded a Purple Heart on or after September 11, 2001, Fry Scholarship recipient, or a transfer-of-entitlement-eligible dependent receiving benefit at the 100% benefit rate.

Visit the Yellow Ribbon webpage at www.va.gov/education/about-gi-bill-benefits/post-9-11/yellow-ribbon-program for additional information about the program and find out if your school is a participant.

Marine Gunnery Sergeant John David Fry Scholarship Eligibility: The Fry Scholarship provides Post-9/11 GI Bill benefits to the children and surviving spouses of Service members who died after September 10, 2001:

- While serving on duty other than active duty as a member of the Armed Forces
- From a service-connected disability while a member of the Selected Reserve

Eligible beneficiaries attending school may receive up to 36 months of benefits at the 100% level. The Fry Scholarship pays full tuition and fees directly to the school for all in-state students at public schools. For those attending private or foreign schools, tuition and fees are capped at a statutory maximum amount per academic year. An MHA and a books and supplies stipend are also paid to the student.

Surviving children who are eligible may begin an approved program of education before the age of 18. A child's marital status has no effect on eligibility. If the qualifying parent's death occurred before January 1, 2013, the child's eligibility ends on their 33rd birthday. If the qualifying parent's death occurred on or after January 1, 2013, the child's eligibility never expires.

Surviving spouses who are eligible have no timeline on when they can use the benefit; however, a spouse will lose eligibility for this benefit upon remarriage.

Edith Nourse Rogers STEM Scholarship: The Edith Nourse Rogers Science, Technology, Engineering and Math (STEM) Scholarship will provide up to nine months of additional benefits (to a maximum of $30,000) to qualifying Veterans and Fry Scholars:

- Seeking a qualifying undergraduate STEM degree alone or as part of a dual-degree program; or
- Have earned a qualifying post-secondary degree or graduate degree and are enrolled in a covered clinical training program for health care professionals; or
- Have earned a qualifying STEM degree and are seeking a teaching certification.

To be eligible, Veterans or Fry Scholars must have exhausted or will exhaust their Post-9/11 GI Bill entitlement within 180 days and must have completed at least 60 semester credit hours (or 90 quarter credit hours) toward their degree already. A qualifying undergraduate STEM program requires at least 120 semesters (or 180 quarter) credit hours for completion or be a teaching certification program. Priority will be given to individuals who are entitled to 100% of Post-9/11 GI Bill benefits and to those who require the most credit hours. The Yellow Ribbon Program may not be used with this extension. Schools may apply Yellow Ribbon funding, but VA cannot match it. These additional benefits cannot be transferred to dependents.

For more information, please visit www.va.gov/education/other-va-education-benefits/stem-scholarship.

Survivor's and Dependents' Educational Assistance (DEA): The DEA program offers education and training opportunities to eligible dependents of Veterans who are (a) permanently and totally disabled due to a service-related condition or (b) died while on active duty or as a result of a service-related condition. Eligible surviving dependents may be eligible for 36 months[2] of degree and certificate courses, apprenticeship, and on-the-job training.

To be eligible, you must be the child or spouse of:

---

2   If benefits were used prior to August 1, 2018, eligible surviving dependents may be eligible for 45 months of benefit entitlement.

44 | Education and Training

- A Veteran who died or is permanently and totally disabled as the result of a service-connected disability. The disability must arise out of active service in the Armed Forces.
- A Veteran who died from any cause while such permanent and total service-connected disability was in existence.
- A Service member missing in action or captured in line of duty by a hostile force.
- A Service member forcibly detained or interned in line of duty by a foreign government or power.
- A Service member who is hospitalized or receiving outpatient treatment for a service-connected permanent and total disability and is likely to be discharged for that disability.

Surviving spouses lose eligibility if they remarry before age 57 or are living with another person who has been recognized publicly as their spouse. They can regain eligibility if their remarriage ends by death or divorce, or if they cease living with the person. Dependent children do not lose eligibility if the surviving spouse remarries.

Visit www.va.gov/education/survivor-dependent-benefits/dependents-education-assistance for more information.

Period of Eligibility: The period of eligibility for Veterans' spouses expires 10 years from either the date they become eligible or the date of the Veteran's death. Children generally must be between the ages of 18 and 26 to receive educational benefits. VA may grant extensions to both spouses and children. The period of eligibility for spouses of Service members who died on active duty expires 20 years from the date of death. Spouses of Service members who died during active duty whose 10-year eligibility period expired before December 10, 2004, have 20 years from the date of death to use educational benefits.

If the event that qualifies a spouse or children for DEA benefits happened to the Veteran or Service member on or after August 1, 2023, the child turned 18 years old on or after August 1, 2023, or the child completed high school or secondary education on or after August 1, 2023, then there are no age or time limits to use DEA benefits if eligible.

Education and Training | 45

Training Available: Benefits may be awarded for pursuit of associate, bachelor, or graduate degrees at colleges and universities; independent study; cooperative training; study abroad; certificate or diploma from business, technical, or vocational schools; apprenticeships; on-the-job training programs; farm cooperative courses; and preparatory courses for tests required or used for admission to an institution of higher learning or graduate school.

Benefits for correspondence courses under certain conditions are available to spouses only. Beneficiaries without high school degrees can pursue secondary schooling. Those with a deficiency in a subject may receive tutorial assistance if enrolled half time or more.

Special Benefits: Dependents over age 14 with physical or mental disabilities that impair their ability to pursue an education may receive specialized vocational or restorative training, including speech and voice correction, language retraining, lip reading, auditory training, Braille reading and writing, and similar programs. Certain disabled or surviving spouses are also eligible.

Montgomery GI Bill Active duty (MGIB-AD): The MGIB-AD (Chapter 30) is an education benefit that provides up to 36 months of education benefits to eligible Veterans and Service members for college degree and certificate programs, technical or vocational courses, flight training, apprenticeships or on-the- job training, high-tech training, licensing and certification testing, entrepreneurship training, certain entrance examinations, and correspondence courses. Remedial, deficiency, and refresher courses may be approved under certain circumstances. Benefits generally expire 10 years after discharge. Current payment rates are available at www.va.gov/education/about-gi-bill-benefits/montgomery-active-duty. Veterans may be eligible for this benefit if they entered active duty after June 30, 1985, are honorably discharged, did not decline MGIB in writing, and served three continuous years of active duty (or have an obligation to serve four years in the Selected Reserve after active-duty service). There are exceptions for disability, re-entering active duty, and upgraded discharges. All participants must have a high school diploma,

46 | Education and Training

equivalency certificate, or have completed 12 hours toward a college degree before applying for benefits.

GI Bill Resident-Rate Requirements: VA must disapprove programs of education at public Institutions of Higher Learning (IHLs) for payment of benefits under the Post-9/11 GI Bill, Montgomery GI Bill-Active duty, and Marine Gunnery Sergeant John David Fry Scholarship programs if the school charges qualifying Veterans and dependents more than the in-state rate for tuition and fees. The student must live in the state where the school is located (regardless of the student's formal state of residence). This requirement is also effective for the payment of benefits under the DEA program.

The in-state tuition provisions do not apply to those individuals on active duty using benefits under the Post-9/11 GI Bill and MGIB-AD.

Application Process: To file online for education benefits, visit www.va.gov/education/how-to-apply.

The following three options are available for Veterans to apply for education benefits:

- Visit your nearest VA regional benefit office (www.benefits. va.gov/benefits/offices.asp) and apply in person.
- Consult with the VA Certifying Official who is usually in the registrar's or financial aid office at the school of your choice. This official has application forms and can help you apply.
- Call 888-GI BILL-1 (888-442-4551) or 1-800-MyVA411 (800-698-2411), option 5 to have the application form mailed to you.

If you wish to find an accredited attorney, claims agent or Veterans Service Officer (VSO) to assist you with your education benefits, you can find a local representative including a recognized VSO, attorney, or claims agent by state/territory, zip code, or by the organization's name online using www.va.gov/ogc/apps/accreditation/index.asp.

Home Loans

Home Loan Guaranty: The VA Home Loan Guaranty program assists eligible Veterans, active-duty Service members, certain surviving spouses, and members of the Reserves and National Guard to obtain, retain and adapt homes in recognition of their service to the nation.

Home Loan Guaranty Uses: A VA loan guaranty helps protect lenders from loss if the borrower fails to repay the loan. It can be used to obtain a loan to buy an existing dwelling or build a home; buy a residential condominium unit; repair, alter or improve a residence owned and occupied by the Veteran; refinance an existing home loan; buy a manufactured home and/or lot; and install a solar heating or cooling system or other energy efficient improvements with a purchase or refinance transaction.

Home Loan Guaranty Eligibility: Eligibility applications can be submitted electronically by going through your lender, who will use the Automated Certificate of Eligibility system. In addition, Veterans can apply through www.va.gov electronically.

It is preferable for lenders and Veterans to apply electronically because most requests submitted using that method are approved instantaneously visiting www.va.gov. However, it is possible to apply for a Certificate of Eligibility (COE) using *VA Form 26-1880, Request for Certificate of Eligibility* or *VA Form 26-1817, Request for Determination of Loan Guaranty Eligibility – Unmarried Surviving Spouses*. Please note that while VA's electronic applications can establish eligibility and issue an online COE in a matter of seconds, the system can only process cases for which VA has enough data in its records. Therefore, certain applicants will not be able to establish eligibility automatically and additional information might be requested prior to the issuance of a COE. If a COE cannot be issued immediately, users have the option of submitting a hardcopy application.

If applying manually for a COE using *VA Form 26-1880*, it is typically necessary that the eligible Veteran present a copy of their report of discharge or DD Form 214, Certificate of Release or Discharge from active duty or other adequate substitute evidence to VA,

48 | Home Loans

which may add significant time to the process. An eligible active-duty Service member should obtain and submit a statement of service signed by an appropriate military official to the appropriate Regional Loan Center mentioned on *VA Form 26-1880*.

A completed *VA Form 26-1880* and any associated documentation should be mailed to the nearest office on the 26-1880. The mailing addresses are located on page 3 of *VA Form 26-1880*, www.vba.va.gov/pubs/forms/vba-26-1880-are.pdf.

For general program information or to obtain VA loan guaranty forms please visit www.benefits.va.gov/homeloans or call 877-827-3702, or 1-800-MyVA411 (800-698-2411), option 5 to reach the home loan program's local office of jurisdiction.

Credit and Income Qualifications: In addition to the periods of eligibility and conditions of service requirements, applicants must have enough income and credit and agree to live in the property to be approved by a lender for a VA home loan.

Surviving Spouses: Some spouses of Veterans may have home loan eligibility, to include:

- The unmarried surviving spouse of a Veteran who died as a result of service or service-connected causes
- The surviving spouse of a Veteran who died on active duty or from service-connected causes, who remarries on or after attaining age 57 and on or after December 16, 2003
- The spouse of an active-duty Service member who is listed as missing in action (MIA) or POW for at least 90 days

For more information, please visit www.benefits.va.gov/homeloans or call 877-827-3702 or 1-800-MyVA411 (800-698-2411), option 5 to speak to a VA home loan representative.

Eligibility under the MIA/POW provision is limited to a one-time use only.

Surviving spouses of Veterans who died from non-service-connected causes may also be eligible if any of the following conditions are met:

- The Veteran was rated totally service-connected disabled for 10 years or more immediately preceding death
- The Veteran was rated totally disabled for not less than five years from date of discharge or release from active duty to date of death
- The Veteran was a former POW who died after September 30, 1999, and was rated totally service-connected disabled for not less than one year immediately preceding death

Home Loan Guaranty Limits: VA does not make guaranteed loans to Veterans and Service members; VA guarantees loans made by private-sector lenders. The guaranty amount is what VA could pay a lender should the loan go to foreclosure or terminate due to a deed in lieu of foreclosure or short sale. On purchase loans, VA limits loan amounts to the lesser of the purchase price or reasonable value as determined by a VA home loan guaranty appraisal plus the VA funding fee. On cash-out refinanced loans, VA limits the loan amount to the reasonable value as determined by a VA home loan guaranty appraisal. VA does not set a cap on how much an individual can borrow to obtain or refinance a home. A lender will evaluate a borrower's credit and income to determine how much they qualify for. In some cases, there are limits on the amount of VA guaranty available due to a current or prior VA-guaranteed home loan, which could affect the amount of money an institution will lend. For information on loan limits please visit www.va.gov/housing-assistance/home-loans/loan-limits.

Other Types of Loans: An eligible borrower can use a VA-guaranteed Interest Rate Reduction Refinancing Loan to refinance an existing VA loan and lower the interest rate and payment.

Home Loan Guaranty Appraisals: In most cases, a home loan cannot be guaranteed by VA without first being appraised by a VA-assigned fee appraiser. A home appraisal by a VA-assigned fee appraiser is required for purchase and certain refinance loans guaranteed by VA. A lender can request a VA appraisal through VA systems. The Veteran borrower typically pays for the appraisal upon completion, according to a fee schedule approved by VA. This VA appraisal estimates the value of the property. An appraisal is not an inspection and does not guarantee the house is free of

Home Loans

defects. VA guarantees the loan, not the condition of the property.

A thorough inspection of the property by a reputable inspection firm may help minimize any problems that could arise after loan closing. In an existing home, attention should be given to plumbing, heating, electrical, roofing, and structural components. In addition, VA strongly recommends testing for radon, a known carcinogen.

Home Loan Guaranty Closing Costs: For purchase home loans, payment in cash is required on all closing costs, including title search, and recording fees, hazard insurance premiums, and prepaid taxes. For refinancing loans, all such costs may be included in the loan, if the total loan does not exceed the reasonable value of the property. Interest rate reduction loans may include closing costs, including a maximum of two discount points.

Home Loan Guaranty Funding Fees: The funding fee is a percentage of the loan amount collected to offset future anticipated costs associated with the loan. A funding fee must be paid to VA unless the Veteran is exempt from such a fee. Currently, exemptions from the funding fee are provided for:

- Veterans and Service members receiving VA service-connected disability compensation

- Those rated by VA as eligible to receive compensation as a result of pre-discharge disability examination and rating

- Those who would be in receipt of compensation, but were recalled to active duty or reenlisted and are receiving active duty pay in lieu of compensation

- Active-duty Service members who have earned a Purple Heart still serving on active duty

- Unmarried surviving spouses in receipt of Dependency and Indemnity Compensation may be exempt

The fee may be paid in cash or included in the loan. For all types of loans, the loan amount may include the VA funding fee and energy efficient improvements up to $3,000 based solely on the documented costs, or up to $6,000, provided the increase in monthly mortgage payments does not exceed the likely reduction in monthly utility costs.

However, no other fees may be included in loans for purchase or construction. This includes fees for the VA appraisal, credit report, loan processing fee, title search, title insurance, recording fees, transfer taxes, survey charges, hazard insurance charges, or discount points. For refinancing loans, most closing costs may be included in the loan amount.

Home Loan Guaranty Required Occupancy: To qualify for a VA home loan, a Veteran, or the spouse of an active-duty Service member must certify that they intend to occupy the home. A dependent child of an active-duty Service member also satisfies the occupancy requirement. When refinancing a VA-guaranteed loan solely to reduce the interest rate, a Veteran only needs to certify prior occupancy.

Home Loan Guaranty Financing, Interest Rates and Terms: Veterans obtain VA-guaranteed loans through external lending institutions, including banks, credit unions, and mortgage brokers. VA-guaranteed loans can have either a fixed interest rate or an adjustable rate, where the interest rate may adjust up to 1% annually and up to 5% over the life of the loan. VA does not set the interest rate. Interest rates and loan terms are negotiable between the lender and borrower on all loan types.

Veterans may also choose a different type of adjustable-rate mortgage (ARM) called a hybrid ARM, where the initial interest rate remains fixed for 3-10 years. If the rate remains fixed for less than five years, the rate adjustment cannot be more than 1% annually and 5% over the life of the loan. For a hybrid ARM with an initial fixed period of five years or more, the initial adjustment may be up to 2%.

The Secretary of VA has the authority to determine annual adjustments thereafter. Currently, annual adjustments may be up to 2 percentage points and 6% over the life of the loan. The term of the loan may be for as long as 30 years and 32 days.

Home Loan Guaranty Assumption Requirements and Liability: VA loans made on or after March 1, 1988, are not assumable without the prior approval of VA, the holder, or its authorized agent (usually the servicer collecting the monthly payments). To

52 | Home Loans

approve the assumption, the holder or servicer must ensure that the purchaser is a satisfactory credit risk and will assume all of the Veteran's liability to the loan. If approved, the purchaser will have to pay a funding fee (unless they are exempt from the VA funding fee) that the lender sends to VA and the Veteran will be released from liability to the federal government. (A VA-guaranteed loan may be assumed by anyone, including non-Veterans.)

Loans made prior to March 1, 1988, are generally freely assumable, but Veterans should still request the lender's approval in order to be released of liability. Veterans whose loans were closed after December 31, 1989, usually have no liability to the government following a foreclosure, except in cases involving fraud, misrepresentation, or bad faith, such as allowing an unapproved assumption. However, for the entitlement to be restored, any loss suffered by VA must be paid in full.

A release of liability does not mean that a Veteran's guaranty entitlement is restored. That occurs only if the borrower is an eligible Veteran who agrees to substitute their entitlement for that of the seller. If the Veteran allows assumptions of a loan without prior approval, then the lender may demand immediate and full payment of the loan and the Veteran may be liable if the loan is foreclosed and VA must pay a claim under the loan guaranty.

VA Assistance to Veterans in Default: When a VA-guaranteed home loan becomes delinquent, VA may provide supplemental servicing to assist Veterans in resolving their mortgage delinquency. The servicer has the primary responsibility of servicing the loan to resolve the default, and VA urges all Veterans who are encountering problems making their mortgage payments to speak with their servicers as soon as possible to explore options to avoid foreclosure.

Contrary to popular opinion, servicers do not want to foreclose, as the foreclosure process becomes very costly. Depending on a Veteran's specific situation, servicers may offer any of the following options to avoid foreclosure:

- **Repayment Plan:** The borrower makes a regular installment each month plus part of the missed installments.

Home Loans | 53

- **Special Forbearance:** The servicer agrees not to initiate foreclosure to allow time for the borrower to repay the missed installments or agrees to place a hold or postpone foreclosures proceedings.

- **Loan Modification:** Provides the borrower a fresh start by adding the delinquency to the loan balance and establishing a new payment schedule.

- **Short Sale:** When the servicer agrees to allow the borrower to sell his/her home for a lesser amount than what is currently required to pay off the loan.

- **Deed-in-Lieu of Foreclosure:** The borrower voluntarily agrees to deed the property to the servicer instead of going through a lengthy foreclosure process. In cases where the servicer is unable to help the Veteran borrower, VA has loan technicians who are available to take an active role in working with the mortgage servicer. Veterans with VA-guaranteed home loans can call 877-827-3702 to discuss their options.

Service members Civil Relief Act (SCRA) and Home Loan Guaranties: Veteran or active-duty borrowers may be able to request relief pursuant to the SCRA. To qualify for certain protections available under the Act, their loan must have originated prior to their current period of active military service. SCRA may provide a lower interest rate during military service and for up to one year after service ends, provide forbearance or prevent foreclosure or eviction up to nine months from period of military service.

Assistance to Veterans with VA-Guaranteed Home Loans: When a VA-guaranteed home loan becomes delinquent, VA may provide supplemental servicing assistance to help cure the default. The servicer has the primary responsibility of servicing the loan to resolve the default.

Veterans with VA-guaranteed home loans can call 877-827-3702 or 1-800-MyVA411 (800-698-2411), option 5 to reach a VA office where loan technicians are prepared to discuss potential ways to help save the loan.

Home Loans

Assistance to Veterans with Non-VA Guaranteed Home Loans: VA advises Veterans or Service members who are having difficulty making payments on a non-VA-guaranteed loan to contact their servicer as quickly as possible to explore options to avoid foreclosure. Although for non-VA loans, VA does not have authority to directly intervene on the borrower's behalf, VA's network of loan technicians can offer advice and guidance on how to potentially avoid foreclosure.

Veterans or Service members with non-VA loans may call 877-827-3702 or 1-800-MyVA411 (800-698-2411), option 5 to speak with a VA loan technician or visit www.benefits.va.gov/homeloans for more information on avoiding foreclosure.

VA Refinancing of a Non-VA Guaranteed Home Loan: Veterans with non-VA guaranteed home loans have the option to refinance to a VA-guaranteed home loan. The Veteran may obtain a VA cash-out refinance for any existing mortgage loan or other indebtedness secured by a lien of record on the home occupied by the Veteran. The amount of the refinancing loan may not exceed 100% of the appraised value of the property. All fees and costs, including the VA funding fee, may be included in the loan amount. However, any portion of fees and costs that would cause the refinancing loan amount to exceed 100% of the appraised value, must be paid in cash at loan closing.

Other Assistance for Delinquent Veteran Borrowers: If VA is not able to help a Veteran borrower retain his/her home (whether a VA-guaranteed loan or not), the Department of Housing and Urban Development (HUD) assists homeowners by sponsoring local housing counseling agencies. To find an approved agency in your area visit www.hud.gov/offices/hsg/sfh/hcc/hcs.cfm or call HUD's interactive voice system at 800-569-4287 to receive assistance in preventing homelessness.

Preventing Veteran Homelessness: Veterans who believe they may be facing homelessness as a result of losing their homes can call 877-4AIDVET (877-424-3838) or 1-800-MyVA411 (800-698-2411), option 6. The service is free, confidential, and is staffed 24/7 with trained counselors who can connect homeless and at- risk Veterans with the nearest VA medical center for help.

Home Loans | 55

VA Acquired Property Sales: VA acquires properties as a result of foreclosures of VA-guaranteed and VA-owned loans. A private contractor currently markets the acquired properties through listing agents using local Multiple Listing Services. A listing of "VA Properties for Sale" may be found at listings.vrmco.com.

Contact a real estate agent for information on purchasing a VA-acquired property.

Loans for Native American Veterans: Eligible Native American Veterans can obtain a direct loan from VA to purchase, construct, or improve a home on federal Trust Land or to reduce the interest rate on such a VA loan. Native American Direct Loans (NADL) are only available if a memorandum of understanding exists between the tribal organization and VA. Veterans who are not Native American, but who are married to Native American non-Veterans, may be eligible for a direct loan under this program.

To be eligible for such a loan, the qualified non-Native American Veteran and the Native American spouse must reside on federal Trust Land, both the Veteran and spouse must have a meaningful interest in the dwelling or lot and the tribal authority that has jurisdiction over the Trust Land must recognize the non-Native American Veteran as subject to its authority. There is no loan limit for Veterans using their entitlement for a NADL to build or purchase a home on Federal trust land.

Eliminating the loan limit enhances access to home loan benefits for Native American Veterans. For additional information about the NADL program visit www.va.gov/housing-assistance/home-loans/loan-types/native-american-direct-loan.

Life Insurance

VA Life Insurance: VA's life insurance benefits that are open to new applicants include Service members' Group Life Insurance (SGLI), Veterans' Group Life Insurance (VGLI), Family Service members' Group Life Insurance (FSGLI), Service members' Group Life Insurance Traumatic Injury Protection (TSGLI), Veterans Affairs Life Insurance (VALife), and Veterans' Mortgage Life Insurance (VMLI).

These programs are described below. Complete details and related forms are available at www.benefits.va.gov/insurance.

You can also find out more about VALife and VMLI by calling VA's Insurance Center at 800-669-8477 or 800-MyVA411 (800-698-2411), option 5 or writing to:

U.S. Department of Veterans Affairs Insurance Center
P.O. Box 42954
Philadelphia, PA 19101

Specialists are available Monday through Friday between 8:30 a.m. and 6 p.m. ET to discuss eligibility, premium payments, insurance dividends, address changes, policy loans, naming beneficiaries, reporting the death of the insured, and other insurance issues.

More information can be obtained from the Office of Service members' Group Life Insurance about VGLI or claims for SGLI and FSGLI by calling 800-419-1473 or writing to:

Office of Service members' Group Life Insurance
P.O. Box 41618
Philadelphia, PA 19176-9913

Specialists are available Monday through Friday between 8 a.m. and 5 p.m. ET to discuss eligibility, premium payments, address changes, naming beneficiaries, reporting the death of the insured, and other insurance issues.

Service members can review and make changes to their SGLI or FSGLI coverage and beneficiaries by accessing the Service members' Online Enrollment System at milconnect.dmdc.osd.mil/milconnect.

Life Insurance | 57

Service members' Group Life Insurance (SGLI): The following persons are automatically insured by law for $500,000 under SGLI:

- Active-duty members of the Army, Navy, Air Force, Marine Corps, Space Force, and Coast Guard
- Commissioned members of the National Oceanic and Atmospheric Administration (NOAA)
- U.S. Public Health Service (UPHS)
- Cadets or midshipmen of the four U.S. military academies (midshipmen/women at the U.S. Merchant Marine Academy are not covered by SGLI)
- Members, cadets, and midshipmen of the Reserved Officers Training Corps (ROTC) while engaged in authorized training and practice cruises
- Members of the Ready Reserves/National Guard who are scheduled to perform at least 12 periods of inactive training per year
- Service members who volunteer for a mobilization category in the Individual Ready Reserve (IRR)

Individuals may elect in the SGLI Online Enrollment System (SOES) or on the SGLV-8286 (only used for part-time members or if SOES access is unavailable) to be covered for less than $500,000 or to decline coverage. SGLI coverage is available in $50,000 increments up to the maximum of $500,000.

Full-time SGLI Coverage: Full-time coverage is in effect during periods of active duty and for Ready Reserve and National Guard members scheduled to perform at least 12 periods of inactive-duty training per year. Coverage is also provided for 120 days after separation or release from duty for Service members who qualify for full-time SGLI coverage at no cost to the Service member. Full-time Service members are covered 24 hours a day, 7 days a week for 365 days of the year.

Part-time SGLI Coverage: Part-time coverage is provided for Reservists or National Guard members who do not qualify for the full-time coverage described above. Part-time coverage generally applies to Reservists/National Guard members who drill only a few

58 | Life Insurance

days in a year. These individuals are covered only while on active duty or active duty for training, or while traveling to and from such duty. Members covered part time do not receive 120 days of free coverage after separation unless they incur or aggravate a disability during a period of duty. For additional information about SGLI coverage, please visit www.va.gov/life-insurance/options-eligibility/sgli.

SGLI Traumatic Injury Protection (TSGLI): TSGLI provides payment to traumatically injured Service members who have suffered certain losses due to traumatic injury. The TSGLI benefit ranges between $25,000 and $100,000, depending on the loss suffered. TSGLI helps service members by providing financial resources that allow their families to be with them during their recovery or by helping them with other expenses incurred during their recovery period.

TSGLI coverage is automatic with SGLI coverage. An additional $1 is added to the Service member's SGLI premium to cover TSGLI. All Service members who are covered by SGLI are automatically also covered by TSGLI. TSGLI cannot be declined unless the Service member also declines basic SGLI. TSGLI claims are adjudicated by the Service member's uniformed service. TSGLI began December 1, 2005, and is retroactive to October 7, 2001; TSGLI coverage is also payable for qualifying injuries incurred during this retroactive period regardless of whether a Service member had SGLI coverage in force at the time of their injury.

For additional information about TSGLI eligibility and uniformed service contact information, go to www.va.gov/life-insurance/options-eligibility/tsgli.

Family Service members' Group Life Insurance Coverage (FSGLI): FSGLI coverage provides coverage to the spouses and dependent children of Service members covered by SGLI. The Service member must pay a premium for spousal coverage. Dependent children are insured at no cost to the Service member.

Spousal Coverage[3]: FSGLI provides up to $100,000 of life

---

3   The insured spouse may convert his or her FSGLI coverage to a permanent policy offered by participating private insurers within 120 days of the date of any of the termination events noted above.

insurance coverage for a spouse of a Service member with full-time SGLI coverage, which cannot exceed the amount of SGLI the Service member has in force. Coverage for civilian spouses is automatic.

For spouses who are in a uniformed service at the same time as the SGLI insured Service member and who got married on or after January 2, 2013, coverage is not automatic. Service members in this category must apply for spousal coverage for their spouse within 240 days from certain events to obtain coverage without a health review. After this time period, they must meet good health requirements to obtain coverage.

Premiums for spousal coverage are based on the age of the spouse and the amount of FSGLI coverage. FSGLI is a Service members' benefit; the member pays the premium and is the sole beneficiary of the coverage.

FSGLI spousal coverage ends due to any of the following events:

- The Service member elects in writing to terminate his or her own SGLI coverage
- The Service member elects in writing to terminate FSGLI coverage on their spouse
- The Service member divorces their spouse
- The Service member dies
- The Service member separates from service

SGLI Online Enrollment System (SOES): All Service members with full-time SGLI coverage can manage their own SGLI coverage and spousal coverage using SOES.

SOES allows Service members with full-time SGLI coverage to make changes to their life insurance coverage and beneficiary information online at any time. To access SOES, the Service member must sign into the MilConnect portal at milconnect.dmdc.osd.mil/milconnect.

Dependent Child Coverage: FSGLI coverage of $10,000 is automatically provided for dependent children of Service members insured under SGLI, at no cost to the Service member.

60 | Life Insurance

FSGLI Dependent Child coverage cannot be declined. FSGLI Dependent Child coverage ends 120 days after any of the following events:

- The Service member elects in writing to decline SGLI coverage
- The child(ren) no longer qualifies as an insurable dependent as defined by 38 U.S.C. 1965
- The Service member dies
- The Service member is discharged from the service

Dependent child coverage cannot be converted to a commercial policy.

For additional information about FSGLI coverage visit www.va.gov/life-insurance/options-eligibility/fsgli.

Veterans' Group Life Insurance (VGLI): VGLI is renewable group term life insurance coverage available to Service members who recently separated from service and had SGLI at the time of separation. Service members have one-year and 120 days fromseparation to apply for VGLI. However, if they apply within 240 days of separation, they do not need to submit evidence of good health. Service members who apply after the 240-day period after separation from service must answer health questions and may be required to submit proof of good health. Veterans can apply online or by completing SGLV 8714. The maximum initial VGLI coverage available is equal to the amount of SGLI coverage held at the time of separation from service.

Effective April 11, 2011, VGLI insureds who are under age 60 and have less than the maximum SGLI coverage allowed by law can purchase up to $25,000 of additional coverage one year after they obtain VGLI and on each subsequent five-year anniversary, up to the current maximum allowed by law or until age 60. No medical underwriting is required for the additional coverage. VGLI is convertible at any time to a permanent plan policy with any participating commercial insurance company.

For additional information about VGLI coverage visit www.va.gov/life-insurance/options-eligibility/vgli.

SGLI Disability Extension: Service members who are totally disabled at the time of separation (i.e., unable to work due to disabilities or have certain statutory conditions), can apply for the SGLI Disability Extension, which provides free coverage for up to two years from the date of separation. To apply, Service members must complete and return SGLV 8715, the SGLI Disability Extension Application. Those covered under the SGLI Disability Extension are automatically converted to VGLI at the end of their extension period, subject to the payment of VGLI premiums. For additional information about the SGLI Disability Extension visit www.va.gov/life-insurance/options-eligibility/sgli.

Accelerated Death Benefits: Like many private life insurance companies, the SGLI, FSGLI, and VGLI programs offer an accelerated benefits option to terminally ill insured members. An insured Service member is considered to be terminally ill if they have a written medical prognosis of nine months or less to live. All terminally ill SGLI and VGLI members are eligible to receive advance payment of up to 50% of their coverage and terminally ill spouses can receive up to 50% of their FSGLI in a lump sum. Payment of an accelerated benefit reduces the amount payable to the beneficiaries at the time of the insured's death.

To apply, an insured member must submit SGLV 8284, Service member/Veteran Accelerated Benefit Option form and spouses must complete SGLV 8284A, Service member Family Coverage Accelerated Benefits Option form.

For additional information about the Accelerated Benefit Option visit www.va.gov/life-insurance/totally-disabled-or-terminally-ill.

Veterans Affairs Life Insurance (VALife): VALife is guaranteed acceptance whole life insurance available to all Veterans aged 80 and under, who have a VA disability rating of 0 to 100%, with no medical underwriting and no time limit to apply. Veterans who are 81 or older and apply for VA Disability Compensation for a service-connected disability before age 81 and receive a rating for that same disability after turning 81 are also eligible if they apply within two years of receiving notification of their rating.

The maximum amount of coverage per applicant is $40,000, with lesser amounts available in $10,000 increments. The face amount of the coverage takes effect two years after the date of enrollment, as long as premiums are paid during the two-year period. This two-year waiting period replaces the need for medical underwriting. If the Insured dies within this two-year period, the beneficiary will receive all premiums paid plus interest.

VALife opened for enrollment effective January 1, 2023, replacing the Service-Disabled Veterans Insurance (S-DVI) program, which closed to new enrollment on December 31, 2022.

NOTE: *Though the S-DVI program is no longer allowing new applications, those currently covered under S-DVI can keep their coverage and may still apply for a waiver of premiums any time after meeting the necessary eligibility requirements.*

For additional information about VALife visit www.va.gov/life-insurance/options-eligibility/valife.

Veterans' Mortgage Life Insurance (VMLI): VMLI is decreasing term mortgage protection insurance available to Service members and Veterans under 70 who have severe service-connected disabilities and receive a Specially Adapted Housing (SAH) Grant from the VA Loan Guaranty Service. SAH Grants help severely disabled Veterans build, remodel, or purchase a home.

Maximum VMLI coverage is the lesser of the existing mortgage balance or $200,000 and is payable only to the mortgage company upon the insured's death. To qualify for VMLI coverage, the Service member or Veteran must meet the following eligibility criteria:

- Be under 70 years of age
- Receive a VA SAH grant for the home;
- Have title to or ownership rights in the home; and
- Have a qualifying mortgage on the home.

VMLI premiums are based on the age of the Service member or Veteran, the length of the mortgage, the balance of the mortgage at the time of application, and the amount of VMLI coverage requested. The Service member/Veteran will need to provide this information to VA to determine the premium. An estimate for premium costs can be obtain by visiting www.insurance.va.gov/vmli/calculator.

VMLI coverage automatically terminates when: 1) the mortgage is paid off in full; 2) ownership in the property secured by the mortgage is terminated; 3) the Service member or Veteran requests termination of coverage; 4) the Service member or Veteran fails to provide required information (i.e., premiums or mortgage information); 5) the premium is not paid; or 6) the Service member or Veteran dies.

If a mortgage is disposed of through sale of the property, VMLI may be requested on the mortgage of another home so long as eligibility requirements are met at the time of the new application.

For additional information about VMLI visit www.va.gov/life-insurance/options-eligibility/vmli.

Additional Life Insurance Program: VA continues to administer several closed life insurance programs for World War II and Korean-Era Veterans with active policies beginning with the letters V, RS, W, J, or JR. Some of these programs offer cash and loan values and some pay dividends. For more information, call 1-800-669-8477.

The loan interest rate is variable and may be obtained by calling 800-669-8477 or 1-800-MyVA411 (800-698-2411), option 5.

Re-Employment Rights

Uniformed Services Re-Employment Rights (includes Reserves and National Guard): The Uniformed Services Employment and Reemployment Rights Act (USERRA) provides for employment and reemployment rights for individuals who left civilian employment to enter service in the uniformed services (either voluntarily or involuntarily). These individuals are entitled to return to reemployment after discharge or release from service if they:

- Gave advance notice of military service to the employer;
- Did not exceed five years cumulative absence from the civilian job (with some exceptions);
- Submitted a timely application for re-employment; and
- Did not receive a dishonorable or other punitive discharge.

The Act provides that a covered individual will be placed into either their previous position or a position that most nearly approximates their previous position as if they had never left, including receiving benefits based on seniority such as pensions, pay increases, and promotions. The Act also prohibits discrimination in hiring, promotion, or other advantages of employment based on military service. Individuals seeking re-employment should apply, verbally or in writing, to the organization's hiring official and keep a record of their application. If problems arise, contact the Department of Labor's Veterans' Employment and Training Service (VETS) in the state of the employer. Federal employees not properly re-employed may appeal directly to the Merit Systems Protection Board. Non-federal employees may file complaints in U.S. District Court. For information, visit www.dol.gov/agencies/vets/programs/userra.

Homelessness Assistance and Prevention

Homeless Veterans: VA's homeless programs constitute the largest integrated network of homeless assistance programs in the country, offering a wide array of services to help Veterans recover from homelessness and live as self-sufficiently and independently as possible. For more information on VA homeless programs and services, Veterans currently enrolled in VA health care can speak with their VA mental health or health care provider. Other Veterans and interested parties can find a complete list of VA health care facilities at www.va.gov/find- locations, or they can call VA's general information hotline at 800-698-2411. If assistance is needed when contacting a VA facility, ask to speak to the Health Care for Homeless Veterans Program or the Mental Health service manager. For additional information please visit www.benefits.va.gov/persona/veteran-homeless.asp or call VA's National Call Center for Homeless Veterans at 877-4AIDVET (877-424-3838).

Homeless Veterans Dental Program (HVDP): The provision of dental care has been shown to significantly improve outcomes related to stable housing, employment, and financial stability for Veterans experiencing homelessness. The HVDP helps increase the accessibility of quality dental care for homeless and certain other Veteran patients enrolled in VA-sponsored and VA partnership homeless rehabilitation programs, namely, the Domiciliary Residential Rehabilitation Treatment, Grant and per Diem, Compensated Work Therapy/Transitional Residence, Healthcare of Homeless Veteran (contract beds), and Community Residential Care programs. For additional information on the Homeless Dental Program please visit www.va.gov/homeless/dental.asp.

Community Resource and Referral Centers (CRRC): CRRCs are a collaborative effort of VA, communities, service providers, and agency partners. CRRCs are centrally located to better engage homeless Veterans. Veterans who enter these centers are referred to physical and mental health care resources, job development programs, housing options, and other VA and non-VA benefits. For more information, please visit www.va.gov/homeless/crrc-list.asp.

VA Health Care for Homeless Veterans (HCHV) Program:

The HCHV Program serves as a gateway to VA and community supportive services for eligible Veterans. This program provides outreach, case management, and HCHV Contract Residential Services (CRS). Whether through referral or direct community outreach, HCHV ensures that homeless Veterans can obtain community-based residential services and facilitates access to programs that provide quality housing and wrap-around services to meet their specialized needs. For additional information, visit www.va.gov/homeless/hchv.asp.

Homeless Veterans Community Employment Services (HVCES):

The mission of HVCES is to provide employment services and resources to Veterans participating in VHA homeless programs to increase access to permanent housing and improve housing stability. Employment decreases the risk of suicide and provides improved quality of life, increased self-confidence and independence, opportunities for socialization, and a decreased reliance on institutional care.

HVCES staff are embedded in homeless programs within the VAMCs, complement existing medical center-based employment services, and are a bridge to employment opportunities and resources in the local community. HVCES is staffed by Vocational Development Specialists and Vocational Rehabilitation Counselors who function as Community Employment Coordinators (CEC) and Employment Specialists.

HVCES provides a range of site-specific employment services rather than being a discrete program. There are no eligibility requirements for Veterans to receive assistance from HVCES other than participation in a VHA homeless program.

For more information about HVCES, visit www.va.gov/homeless/hvces.asp.

Homeless Patient Aligned Care Team (HPACT):

HPACTs provide a coordinated "medical home" designed around the unique needs and distinct challenges homeless Veterans face both accessing and engaging in health care. At selected VA facilities, Veterans are assigned to an HPACT that includes a primary care provider, nurse, social worker, homeless program staff, and others who offer medical care, case management, outreach, housing assistance, and social services. HPACT provides and coordinates the health care that Veterans may need while helping them obtain and stay in permanent housing. In FY 2023, 25 HPACT teams were awarded a Mobile Medical Unit (MMU) equipped to bring health care and supportive services directly to Veterans experiencing homelessness in the community setting. As of April 2024, all 25 MMUs have been deployed to the awarded sites. For more information, visit www.va.gov/homeless/hpact.asp.

Homeless Providers Grant and Per Diem Program (GPD): The GPD program allows VA to award grants to community-based agencies to create transitional housing programs with wrap-around supportive services to assist vulnerable Veterans move into permanent housing. The GPD program is VA's largest transitional housing program with approximately 11,000 beds nationwide.

The purpose of the program is to meet Veterans at various stages as they move to stable housing. Community-based organizations offer focused services through a variety of transitional housing models targeted to different populations and needs of Veterans. The GPD program plays a vital role in the continuum of homeless services by providing support to those Veterans who otherwise would be among the unsheltered homeless population. The result of GPD programs is that Veterans achieve residential stability, increase their skill levels and/or income, and obtain greater self-determination. For more information and a list of GPD grantee locations, visit www.va.gov/homeless/gpd.asp or visit Grants.gov for GPD's forecast.

Housing and Urban Development-Veterans Affairs Supportive Housing (HUD-VASH) Program: This collaborative program pairs HUD's Housing Choice Voucher rental assistance with VA case management and supportive services. These services are designed to help homeless Veterans and their families obtain permanent housing and access the health care, mental health treatment, and other supports necessary to help them improve their quality of life and maintain housing over time. For more information, please visit www.va.gov/homeless/hud-vash.asp.

Homelessness Assistance and Prevention

Supportive Services for Veterans Families (SSVF) Program: The SSVF Program provides supportive services to very low- income Veteran families living in or transitioning to permanent housing. SSVF is designed to rapidly rehouse homeless Veteran families and prevent homelessness for those at imminent risk of becoming homeless due to a housing crisis. Funds are granted to private nonprofit organizations and consumer cooperatives, which then provide very low-income Veteran families with a range of supportive services designed to promote housing stability. For more information, visit www.va.gov/homeless/ssvf/index.html.

In addition, to help families respond to affordable housing challenges, SSVF's Shallow Subsidy services provide Veteran families with a fixed rental subsidy for up to two years with a goal of achieving long-term self-sufficiency through employment. Additionally, grantees were provided authorities to allow incentives to support placements into permanent housing. For more information and a list of SSVF grantee locations, visit www.va.gov/homeless/ssvf/index.html.

Domiciliary Care for Homeless Veterans (DCHV): This program is for Veterans with mental health concerns who are homeless, at risk for homelessness, or otherwise lacking a stable lifestyle or living arrangement that is conducive to their goal of recovery. Care is provided for multiple challenges, illnesses, or rehabilitative needs. When Veterans finish the residential program, they are discharged to appropriate safe housing.

Compensated Work Therapy-Transitional Residence: Designed for Veterans who face employment barriers due to mental health conditions or physical disabilities, Compensated Work Therapy-Transitional Residence (CWT-TR) provides Veterans with assistance and coaching to find and retain jobs as they continue treatment, empowering their transition to independent living. CWT-TR homes are often located in the community, providing a transitional home for Veterans as they work toward successful integration into the community. Veterans pay a program fee, derived from their CWT-related earnings, to help cover residential costs.

Family Members/Survivors

Key Information for Family Members about the Affordable Care Act: The Affordable Care Act was created to expand access to affordable health care coverage to all Americans, lower costs, and improve quality and care coordination. Under the health care law, people will have health coverage that meets a minimum standard (called "minimum essential coverage") by January 1, 2014, or pay a fee when filing their taxes, if they have affordable options but remain uninsured (unless they qualify for an exemption).

VA wants all Veterans and their families to receive health care that improves their health and well-being. Dependents and survivors enrolled in the Civilian Health and Medical Program of the U.S. Department of Veterans Affairs (CHAMPVA), or the Spina Bifida Health Care Program, meet the requirement to have health care coverage under the health care law and do not need to take any additional steps. The law does not change CHAMPVA or Spina Bifida benefits, access, or costs. Veterans' family members who do not have the minimum essential coverage required by the health law may shop for and purchase private health insurance through the Health Insurance Marketplace.

For more information about the Health Insurance Marketplace, visit www.healthcare.gov or call 800-318-2596. For additional information about the VA and the health care law, visit www. va.gov/health-care/about-affordable-care-act or call 877-222-VETS (877-222-8387) or 1-800-MyVA411 (800-698-2411), option 2.

Dependents and Survivors Benefits: Death Gratuity: The death gratuity program provides for a special tax-free payment of $100,000 to eligible survivors of members of the Armed Forces, who die while on active duty or while serving in certain reserve statuses. The death gratuity is the same regardless of the cause of death.

The longstanding purpose of the death gratuity has been to provide immediate cash payment to assist survivors of deceased members of the Armed forces to meet their financial needs during the period immediately following a member's death and before other survivor benefits, if any, become available.

70 | Family Members/Survivors

For eligibility and program information about the DoD Death Gratuity benefit visit militarypay.defense.gov/Benefits/Death-Gratuity.

Survivor Benefit Program: The Survivor Benefit Plan is a Department of Defense sponsored and subsidized program that provides up to 55 percent of a service member's retired pay to an eligible beneficiary upon the death of the member. The program provides no-cost automatic coverage to members serving on active duty, and reserve component members who die of a service-connected cause while performing inactive duty training. In addition, active-duty members can purchase coverage upon retirement and reserve component members can elect coverage when they have 20 years of qualifying service for reserve retired pay.

For additional information about the DoD Survivor benefit program visit militarypay.defense.gov/Benefits/Survivor-Benefit-Program.

Dependency and Indemnity Compensation (DIC): DIC is a tax-free monetary benefit generally payable to eligible survivors of military service members who died in the line of duty or eligible survivors of Veterans whose death resulted from a service-related injury or disease. DIC may also be paid to certain survivors of Veterans who were totally disabled from service-connected conditions at the time of death, even though their service-connected disabilities did not cause their deaths. The survivor qualifies if the Veteran was:

- Continuously rated totally disabled for a period of 10 years immediately preceding death; or
- Continuously rated totally disabled from the date of military discharge and for at least 5 years immediately preceding death; or
- A former POW who was continuously rated totally disabled for a period of at least one year immediately preceding death.

For more detailed information, visit www.va.gov/disability/survivor-dic-rates.

Family Members/Survivors | 71

DIC Eligibility (Surviving Spouse): To qualify for DIC, a surviving spouse must meet the following requirements:

- Married to a service member who died on active duty, active duty for training, or inactive duty training; or
- Validly married the Veteran before January 1, 1957; or
- Married the Veteran within 15 years of discharge from the period of military service in which the disease or injury that caused the Veteran's death began or was aggravated; or
- Was married to the Veteran for a least one year; or
- Had a child with the Veteran and cohabitated with the Veteran continuously until the Veteran's death; or
- If separated, was not at fault for the separation and is not currently remarried.

NOTE: A surviving spouse who remarries on or after January 5, 2021, upon attaining age 55 remains eligible for DIC benefits. A surviving spouse who previously lost eligibility to DIC due to a remarriage occurring between the ages of 55 and 57, would now be eligible to have the benefit reinstated effective January 5, 2021.

DIC Eligibility (Surviving Child): A surviving child may be eligible if not included on the surviving spouse's DIC and is unmarried and under age 18 or between the ages of 18 and 23 and attending school at an approved institution.

NOTE: A child adopted out of the Veteran's family may be eligible for DIC if all other eligibility criteria are met.

DIC Eligibility (Surviving Parent): Parents' DIC is an income-based benefit for parents who were financially dependent on a Service member or Veteran who died from a service-related cause. When countable income exceeds the limit set by law, no benefits are payable. The spouse's income must also be included if the parent is living with a spouse.

DIC and Aid and Attendance/Housebound Benefits: If a Veteran died on or after January 1, 1993, the Veteran's surviving spouse may receive additional benefits beyond the basic DIC rate if the spouse is residing in a skilled nursing facility, require the regular

72 | Family Members/Survivors

assistance of another person to perform the activities of daily living or if they are permanently housebound. This additional benefit is referred to as "Aid and Attendance" or "Housebound."

DIC 8-Year Special Allowances: If a deceased Veteran was considered "permanent and totally disabled" (either by 100% rating or permanent and total individual unemployability) for eight (8) continuous years prior to death and the surviving spouse was married to the Veteran for those same eight years, the surviving spouse may be entitled to an additional monthly benefit on the DIC award. If there are any surviving dependent children under age 18 in the care of the surviving spouse, an additional child supplement payment may be further added to the DIC award for the initial two (2) years of entitlement. This additional amount will be automatically terminated two years after the DIC award grant.

Restored Entitlement Program for Survivors: An additional special benefit may be payable to Survivors of a Veteran who died of service-connected causes prior to August 13, 1981. The amount of the benefit is based on information provided by the Social Security Administration.

Survivors Pension: Survivors Pension is an income and net worth-based program payable to low-income surviving spouses or children who have not married/remarried since the death of the Veteran. Any benefit payable is reduced by annual income from other sources, such as Social Security. If the Survivor has unreimbursed medical expenses, these costs can be deducted from countable income to increase the benefit amount (such as cost of care at an Assisted Living or Skilled Nursing Facility). For additional information on pension benefits please visit www. va.gov/pension/survivors-pension.

Eligibility for Survivors Pension: To be eligible for Survivor's Pension, the deceased Veteran must have met the following requirements:

- If the Veteran served on or before September 7, 1980, the Veteran must have served at least 90 days of active military service, with at least one day during a wartime period
- If the Veteran entered active duty after September 7, 1980, the

Veteran generally must have served at least 24 months or the full tour of duty with at least one day during a wartime period

- Discharged from military service under other than dishonorable conditions

To qualify as a surviving child of a deceased Veteran, the child must meet the following requirements: under age 18 (or under age 23 if attending a VA-approved school) or permanently incapable of self-support due to a disability diagnosed before age 18.

How to Apply for Survivors Pension: To apply for Survivors Pension, download and complete *VA Form 21P 534EZ, "Application for DIC, Death Pension, and/or Accrued Benefits."* You can mail your application to the address below:

Pension Intake Center
P.O. Box 5365
Janesville, WI 53547

Survivors Aid and Attendance and Housebound Benefits: Survivors who are eligible for pension and require the aid and attendance of another person, or are housebound, may be eligible for a higher maximum annual pension rate. These benefits are paid in addition to monthly pension, and they are not paid without eligibility to survivor's pension. Since aid and attendance and housebound allowances increase the pension amount, people who are not eligible for a basic pension due to excessive income may be eligible for pension at these increased rates. A surviving spouse may not receive aid and attendance benefits and housebound benefits at the same time. For additional information on aid and attendance and housebound benefits including how to apply please visit www.va.gov/pension/aid-attendance-housebound.

To apply for aid and attendance or housebound benefits, submit a *VA Form 21-2680, Examination for Housebound Status or Permanent Need for Regular Aid and Attendance* to the address shown below:

U.S. Department of Veterans Affairs
Pension Intake Center
P.O. Box 5365
Janesville, WI 53547

74 | Family Members/Survivors

Please include copies of any evidence, preferably a report from an attending physician or a nursing home, validating the need for aid and attendance or housebound status. The report should contain enough detail to determine whether there is disease or injury producing physical or mental impairment, loss of coordination or conditions affecting the ability to dress and undress, to feed oneself, to attend to sanitary needs, and to keep oneself ordinarily clean and presentable; or whether confined to the immediate premises due to disability.

Reductions for Medicaid Covered Nursing Facility Care: Surviving spouses without dependents or surviving children who are in a Medicaid-approved nursing facility and are covered by a Medicaid plan for services furnished by the nursing facility are limited to receiving $90 per month in pension benefits. No part of the $90 monthly pension may be used to reduce the amount of Medicaid paid to a nursing facility.

Children of Women Vietnam Veterans Born with Certain Birth Defects: Biological children of women Veterans who served in Vietnam at any time during the period beginning on February 28, 1961, and ending on May 7, 1975, may be eligible for certain benefits because of birth defects associated with the mother's service in Vietnam that resulted in a permanent physical or mental disability.

The covered birth defects do not include conditions due to family disorders, birth-related injuries or fetal or neonatal infirmities with well-established causes. A monetary allowance is paid at one of four disability levels based on the child's degree of permanent disability. For more information, visit www.va.gov/disability/eligibility/special-claims/birth-defects.

Office of Survivors Assistance: VA has an Office of Survivors Assistance (OSA) that serves as information experts about the benefits available for survivors. You can contact them with questions at officeofsurvivors@va.gov. For more information, visit www.va.gov/survivors.

Appeals and Supplemental Claims

Disagreements With VA Claims Decisions Under Appeals Modernization: The Veteran Appeals Improvement and Modernization Act of 2017, implemented on February 19, 2019, modernized the claims and appeals process. The modernized appeals process is simple, timely and fair to Veterans, offering Veterans greater choice in how they resolve disagreements with VA decisions.

Typical decisions subject to review include disability compensation, pension, education benefits, recovery of overpayments, reimbursement for unauthorized medical services, and denial of burial and memorial benefits. A claimant generally has one year from the date of the notice of a VA decision to request a decision review from one of three options. However, claimants only have 60 days to file an appeal for contested claims (claims where a favorable decision on one claim requires the denial or a lesser benefit to another claimant). Appeals for contested claims must be filed directly with the Board of Veterans' Appeals (Board).

To file a disagreement with a VA decision dated on or after February 19, 2019, Veterans or claimants may pursue one of three different options: a higher-level review, supplemental claim, or an appeal directly to the Board.

Supplemental Claim: A claimant may file a supplemental claim using *VA Form 20-0995, Decision Review Request: Supplemental Claim*, available at www.vba.va.gov/pubs/forms/VBA-20-0995-ARE. pdf. Claimants must be sure to identify or submit new and relevant evidence. New evidence means evidence not previously part of the actual record before agency adjudicators at the time of the prior decision. Relevant evidence means evidence that tends to prove or disprove a matter at issue in a claim. Claimants may file supplemental claims at any time; however, filing the request within one year of the date of notice of the prior decision on the issue(s) maintains potential entitlement to the earliest possible effective date, if VA is able to grant the benefit. For more information, visit www.va.gov/decision-reviews/supplemental-claim.

76 | Appeals and Supplemental Claims

Higher-Level Review: A claimant may request a higher-level review (HLR) using *VA Form 20-0996, Decision Review Request: Higher-Level Review*, available at www.va.gov/decision-reviews/higher-level-review/request-higher-level-review-form-20-0996/start. With an HLR, an experienced VA adjudicator, who did not participate in the prior decision, reexamines the same evidence used in the prior decision, and decides the claim without considering that prior decision. The claimant and/or representative may request one informal conference with the higher-level reviewer to identify any errors in law or fact VA made in the prior decision.

VA must receive the completed *VA Form 20-0996* within one year of the date of the notification letter of the prior decision. A claimant may request an HLR for most decisions, except immediately following an HLR or a Board decision involving the same issue.

For HLRs and supplemental claims, mail forms to:

Disability compensation
Department of Veterans Affairs
Claims Intake Center
PO Box 4444
Janesville, WI 53547-4444

Life insurance
Department of Veterans Affairs
Attention: Insurance Center
PO Box 5209
Janesville, WI 53547

Pension and survivor benefits
Department of Veterans Affairs
Claims Intake Center
PO Box 5365
Janesville, WI 53547-5365

All other benefit types

Check the decision letter for your initial claim for instructions on how to submit the form.

Appeals and Supplemental Claims | 77

Appeal to the Board of Veterans' Appeals (Board): A Veteran or claimant may appeal directly to the Board using *VA Form 10182, Decision Review Request: Board Appeal (Notice of Disagreement)* within one year of the date of the VA decision.

Veterans or claimants appealing to the Board may request a hearing with a Veterans law judge and/or have the opportunity to submit additional evidence. The Board can also conduct a review without any additional evidence, which could result in a faster decision. *VA Form 10182* should be submitted to:

> Board of Veterans' Appeals
> P.O. Box 27063
> Washington DC 20038
>
> or by fax: 844-678-8979

A Board decision under the modernized program also may be appealed to the U.S. Court of Appeals for Veterans Claims.

For additional information on the decision review and appeals processes or to download the appropriate request forms, visit www.va.gov/decision-reviews.

Legacy Appeals: For VA decisions issued prior to February 19, 2019, under the legacy appeals process, a claimant had one year from the date of the notification of a VA decision to file an appeal by filing a written notice of disagreement with the VA department that made the decision. There are still some cases pending in the legacy appeals system.

In the legacy appeals system, following the receipt of the claimant's written notice, VA issues the claimant a "Statement of the Case" (SOC) describing the facts, laws and regulations used in deciding the case. To complete the request for appeal, the claimant must file a "Substantive Appeal" or *VA Form 9* , available at www. va.gov/vaforms/va/pdf/VA9.pdf within 60 days of the mailing of the SOC, or within one year from the date VA mailed its decision, whichever period ended later.

Claimants with a pending legacy appeal can opt-in to the modernized appeals system when they receive an SOC or a

78 | Appeals and Supplemental Claims

Supplemental Statement of the Case (SSOC). To opt-in, claimants must submit the required form, electing to opt-in to the modernized appeals process within 60 days from the date of the SOC/SSOC or within the one-year appeal period. For further information on opting in and to locate the applicable forms, visit www.benefits.va.gov/benefits/appeals.asp.

Board of Veterans' Appeals: The Board decides appeals on behalf of the Secretary of Veterans Affairs. Although it is not required, a VSO, an accredited agent, or attorney may represent a claimant. Appellants who wish to have a hearing may present their cases in person to a member of the Board in Washington, D.C., at a VA regional office or by videoconference. Decisions made by the Board on your case can be found by logging into www.va.gov.

The pamphlet, "How Do I Appeal," is available on the Board of Veterans' Appeals website, www.bva.va.gov, or may be requested by writing:

> Mail Process Section (014)
> Board of Veterans' Appeals
> 810 Vermont Avenue, NW
> Washington, DC 20420

U.S. Court of Appeals for Veterans Claims: A final Board decision that does not grant a claimant the benefits desired may be appealed to the U.S. Court of Appeals for Veterans Claims. The court is an independent body, not part of VA.

Notice of an appeal must be received by the court with a postmark that is within 120 days after the Board mailed its decision. The court reviews the record considered by the Board. It does not hold trials or receive new evidence. Appellants may represent themselves before the court or have lawyers or approved agents as representatives. Oral argument is held only at the direction of the court. Either party may appeal a decision of the court to the U.S. Court of Appeals for the Federal Circuit and may seek review in the U.S. Supreme Court. Published decisions, case status information, rules and procedures, and other special announcements can be found at www.uscourts.cavc.gov. For questions, call 202-501-5970 or write to:

Clerk of the Court
625 Indiana Ave. NW, Suite 900
Washington, DC 20004

Correcting Military Records: The Secretary of a military department, acting through a Board for Correction of Military Records, has the authority to change any military record when necessary to correct an error or remove an injustice. A correction board may consider applications for correction of a military record, including a review of a discharge issued by court-martial. All branches of the military consider you to have a strong case for a discharge upgrade if you can show your discharge was connected to any of these categories:

- Mental health conditions, including posttraumatic stress disorder (PTSD)
- Traumatic brain injury (TBI)
- Sexual assault or harassment during military service, military sexual trauma (MST)
- Sexual orientation (including under the Don't Ask, Don't Tell policy)

For more information, please visit www.va.gov/discharge-upgrade-instructions. Application is made with DD Form 149, available at VA offices, Veterans organizations or visit www.esd.whs.mil/Directives/forms/dd1000_1499.

Review of Discharge from Military Service: Each of the military services maintains a discharge review board with authority to change correct or modify discharges or dismissals not issued by a sentence of a general court-martial. The board has no authority to address medical discharges. If the Veteran is deceased or incompetent, the surviving spouse, next of kin, or legal representative they may apply for a review of discharge by writing to the military department concerned, using DD Form 293, "Application for the Review of Discharge from the Armed Forces of the United States." This form may be obtained at a VA regional office, from Veterans organizations or online at www.esd.whs.mil/Directives/forms/dd1000_1499.

80 | Appeals and Supplemental Claims

However, if the discharge was more than 15 years ago, a Veteran must petition the appropriate Service's Board for Correction of Military Records using *DD Form 149, "Application for Correction of Military Records Under the Provisions of Title 10, U.S. Code, Section 1552."* A discharge review is conducted by a review of an applicant's record and, if requested, by a hearing before the board.

Discharges awarded because of a continuous period of unauthorized absence in excess of 180 days make persons ineligible for VA benefits regardless of action taken by discharge review boards, unless VA determines there were compelling circumstances for the absence. Boards for the Correction of Military Records may also consider such cases. Veterans with disabilities incurred or aggravated during active duty may qualify for medical or other benefits regardless of separation and characterization of service. Veterans separated administratively under other than honorable conditions may request that their discharge be reviewed for possible recharacterization, provided they file their appeal within 15 years of the date of separation. Questions regarding the review of a discharge should be addressed to the appropriate discharge review board at the address listed on DD Form 293.

Physical Disability Board of Review: Veterans separated due to disability from September 11, 2001, through December 31, 2009, with a combined rating of 20% or less, as determined by the respective branch of service Physical Evaluation Board (PEB) and not found eligible for retirement, may be eligible for a review by the Physical Disability Board of Review (PDBR).

The PDBR was established to reassess the accuracy and fairness of certain PEB decisions and, where appropriate, recommend the correction of discrepancies and errors. A PDBR review will not lower the disability rating previously assigned by the PEB and any correction may be made retroactively to the day of the original disability separation. As a result of the request for review by the PDBR, no further relief from the Board of Corrections of Military Records may be sought and the recommendation by the PDBR, once accepted by the respective branch of service, is final.

Burial and Memorial Benefits

VA operates 155 national cemeteries, of which more than 95 are open to interments of either casket or cremains. Burial options are limited to those available at a specific cemetery and may include in-ground casket or interment of cremated remains in a columbarium, in ground, or in a scattering area. For more information, visit the National Cemetery Administration website at www.cem.va.gov.

Burial in VA National Cemeteries

Eligibility: Burial in a national cemetery is open to all members of the Armed Forces and Veterans who have met minimum active-duty service requirements and were discharged under conditions other than dishonorable. Veterans married to Veterans are entitled to their own adjacent gravesites if they choose.

Members of the Reserve components of the Armed Forces who die while on active duty or on training duty, were eligible for retired pay, or were called to active duty and served the full term of service for which they were called, may also be eligible for burial.

Their surviving spouse, minor children, and, under certain conditions, unmarried adult children with disabilities, may also be eligible for burial. Eligible spouses and children may be buried even if they predecease the Veteran. The Veteran and eligible family members typically share the same gravesite or columbarium niche, allowing all family members to be interred together.

With certain exceptions, eligibility for burial based on active-duty service must have been for a minimum of 24 consecutive months beginning after September 7, 1980 (for an enlisted person) or after October16, 1981 (for officers). In the case of reservists or National Guard members called to active duty for a limited duration, they must have served the full period for which they were ordered to active duty. Active duty for training, by itself, while serving in the Reserves or National Guard, is not sufficient to establish eligibility. Reservists and National Guard members, as well as their spouses and dependent children, are eligible if they were entitled to retired pay at the time of death or would have been upon reaching the requisite age.

82 | Burial and Memorial Benefits

VA may bar eligible individuals from receiving burial and memorial benefits if they are convicted of a Federal or State capital crime or a Federal or State crime that caused the person to be a tier III sex offender; or, if the individual committed such an offense, but was not convicted of such crime because the person was not available for trial due to death or flight to avoid prosecution. Such benefits include burial in a VA national cemetery and receipt of a government-furnished headstone, marker, medallion, burial flag, and Presidential Memorial Certificate. Veterans and other claimants for VA burial benefits have the right to appeal decisions made by VA regarding eligibility for burial and memorial benefits. For more information about the appeals process, contact the nearest VA national cemetery listed at www.cem.va.gov/cem/cems/listcem.asp or call 800-827-1000 or 1-800-MyVA411 (800-698-2411), option 4.

Surviving spouses of Veterans who died on or after January 1, 2000, do not lose eligibility for burial in a national cemetery if they remarry.

Unmarried dependent children of Veterans who are under 21 years of age, or under 23 years of age if a full-time student at an approved educational institution, are eligible for burial. Unmarried adult children who become physically or mentally disabled and incapable of self-support under age 21, or under age 23 if a full-time student, may also be eligible.

Certain parents of service members who die due to hostile activity or from combat training-related injuries may be eligible for burial in a national cemetery with their child. The biological or adoptive parents of a Service member who died in combat or while performing training in preparation for a combat mission, who leaves no surviving spouse or dependent child, may be buried with the deceased Service member if there is available space.

Eligibility is limited to those who died on or after October 7, 2001, and biological or adoptive parents who died on or after October 13, 2010.

The next of kin or authorized representative, such as the funeral director, may make interment arrangements at the time of need by contacting the National Cemetery Scheduling Office

Burial and Memorial Benefits | 83

At 800-535-1117, or 1-800-MyVA411 (800-698-2411), option 4, in some cases, the national cemetery in which burial is desired. VA does not normally conduct burials on weekends. Gravesites cannot be reserved, except for Veterans married to each other, who may choose to be interred together or may reserve an adjacent gravesites/columbarium niche after the first interment is made. VA will honor reservations made before 1973 by the Department of the Army.

Pre-Need Burial Eligibility Determination: VA implemented the Pre-need Burial Eligibility Determination Program to assist individuals interested in determining their eligibility for burial in a VA national cemetery.

Through this program, Veterans and their eligible family members can plan to use VA burial benefits that Veterans have earned through their military service. Planning in advance for a Veteran's or loved-one's final resting place can eliminate unnecessary delays during a family's time of bereavement. Veteran families will have increased confidence that their loved ones are eligible for burial in a VA national cemetery at their time of need.

To apply, individuals must submit *VA Form 40-10007, Application for Pre-Need Determination of Eligibility for Burial* in a VA National Cemetery (available at www.va.gov/vaforms), to the National Cemetery Scheduling Office by faxing to 855-840-8299 or by mailing to:

NCA Intake Center
P.O. Box 5237
Janesville, WI 53547

For more details, or to apply online, visit www.cem.va.gov/cem/pre-need/index.asp.

Burial Headstones and Markers: VA is authorized to furnish, upon request, an inscribed headstone or marker for the unmarked grave of an eligible decedent at any national, state Veterans, tribal, or private cemetery. VA will deliver a headstone or marker at no cost, anywhere in the world. For Medal of Honor (MOH) recipients, VA is authorized to provide a supplemental headstone or marker if the recipient served in the Armed Forces on or after April 6, 1917,

84 | Burial and Memorial Benefits

and is eligible for a headstone or marker (or would be but for the individual's date of death), even if the grave is already marked with a private headstone or marker. For eligible Veterans (who are not Medal of Honor recipients) buried in a private cemetery whose deaths occurred on or after November 1, 1990, VA may furnish a government headstone or marker even if the grave is already marked with a private one.

Spouses and dependent children are eligible to have inscription information (e.g., HIS WIFE, HER HUSBAND, HUSBAND OF, SPOUSE OF) on a Veteran's government headstone or marker if the Veteran died on or after October 16, 2019 and is buried in private cemetery.

Before requesting a headstone or marker for use in a private cemetery, eligible applicants should check with the cemetery to ensure the government-furnished headstone or marker will be accepted.

Those who may apply for burial headstones and markers include

- The decedent's spouse or individual in a legal union with the decedent
- The decedent's child, parent, or sibling, whether biological; adopted or step relation
- Any lineal or collateral descendant of the decedent
- Personal representative from a VSO
- Individual employed by state or local government responsible for serving Veteran
- Individual with legal responsibility for the disposition of the unclaimed remains of the decedent or other matters related to interment or memorialization
- Anyone – if the decedent's dates of service ended prior to April 6, 1917 (applies to others whose eligibility is derived)

All installation fees at private cemeteries are the responsibility of the applicant.

Memorial Markers: VA provides memorial headstones and markers for placement in a national cemetery, a Veterans cemetery owned by a state, or (in the case of a Veteran) in a state, tribal,

Burial and Memorial Benefits | 85

local, or private cemetery with "IN MEMORY OF" as the first line of inscription for those whose remains are unavailable for burial. Remains that are unavailable for burial are those that have not been recovered or identified, were buried at sea, donated to science or cremated and scattered completely. Only eligible Veterans are authorized to receive memorial headstones or markers for use in private cemeteries.

Spouses or surviving spouses and dependent children of a Veteran or Service member serving on active duty under conditions other than dishonorable, who die on or after November 11, 1998, and before October 1, 2024, may be eligible to receive a memorial headstone or marker for placement in a national cemetery, Veterans' cemetery owned by a state, or a Veterans' cemetery of a Tribal Organization on land owned by or held in trust for a Tribal Organization. Eligible dependent children of Veterans or Service members must be under age 21 years or under the age of 23 years if pursuing a course of instruction at an approved educational institution or are unmarried and became permanently physically or mentally disabled and incapable of self-support before reaching age 21 years, or before reaching 23 years if pursuing a course of instruction at an approved educational institution.

To submit a claim for a headstone or marker, or for a memorial marker for placement in a private cemetery, use *VA Form 40-1330, Claim for Standard Government Headstone or Marker* (available at www.va.gov/vaforms) and provide a copy of the Veteran's military discharge documents or proof of military service. Claims sent without supporting documents may be delayed until eligibility can be determined. Upload the application packet via eauth.va.gov/accessva or mail the completed form and supporting documents to:

NCA FP Evidence Intake Center
P.O. Box 5237
Janesville, WI 53547

The form and supporting documents may also be faxed toll-free to 800-455-7143.

Inscriptions: Headstones and markers must be inscribed with the name of the deceased, branch of service, and year of birth and

86 | Burial and Memorial Benefits

death. They also may be inscribed with other optional information, including an emblem of belief, and, space permitting, additional text including military rank; war service such as "WORLD WAR II"; complete date of birth and death; military awards; military organizations; civilian or Veteran affiliations; and personalized words of endearment.

Medallion in Lieu of Government Headstone or Marker for Private Cemeteries: For decedents who served in the U.S. Armed Forces on or after April 6, 1917, and are eligible for VA memorialization benefits (or would be but for date of death), VA is authorized to provide a medallion instead of a headstone or marker if the grave is in a private cemetery and already marked with a privately purchased headstone or marker. The VA medallion denotes the decedents' status as a Veteran. The Medal of Honor Medallion is inscribed with "MEDAL OF HONOR" at the top and the branch of service at the bottom.

To submit a claim for a medallion to be affixed to a private headstone or marker in a private cemetery, use *VA Form 40-1330M, Claim for Government Medallion for Placement in A Private Cemetery* (available at www.va.gov/vaforms), and provide a copy of the Veteran's military discharge documents or proof of military service. Claims sent without supporting documents may be delayed until eligibility can be determined.

Upload the application packet via eauth.va.gov/accessva or mail the completed form and supporting documents to:

NCA FP Evidence Intake Center
P.O. Box 5237
Janesville, WI 53547

The form and supporting documents may also be faxed toll-free to 800-455-7143.

To check the status of a claim for a headstone or marker for placement in a national, state, or tribal Veterans cemetery, please call that cemetery. To check the status of one being placed in a private cemetery, please contact the Applicant Assistance Unit at 800-697-6947.

Burial and Memorial Benefits | 87

Other Memorialization

Presidential Memorial Certificates (PMCs): PMCs are issued to honor the memory of deceased persons whom VA finds eligible for burial in a national cemetery. This includes persons who died on active military, naval or air service; members of Reserve components of the Armed Forces, including Army or Air National Guard; members of the Army, Navy, or Air Force Reserve Officers' Training Corps; or persons who at death were entitled to retired pay or would have been but for age.

Eligible recipients, including the next of kin, a relative, friend or authorized service representative may request a PMC by submitting a completed and signed *VA Form 40-0247, Presidential Memorial Certificate Request Form*, along with a copy of the Veteran's military discharge document or proof of military service to:

NCA FP Evidence Intake Center
P.O. Box 5237
Janesville, WI 53547

The form and supporting documents may also be faxed toll-free to 800-455-7143 or submitted electronically at www.va.gov/burials-memorials/memorial-items/presidential-memorial-certificates.

Requests sent without supporting documents may be delayed until eligibility can be determined. More information can be found at www.cem.va.gov/cem/pmc.asp.

Burial Flags: VA will furnish a U.S. burial flag to recognize deceased Veterans who received other than dishonorable discharge. This includes certain persons who served in the organized military forces of the Commonwealth of the Philippines while in service of the U.S Armed Forces and who died on or after April 25, 1951. Also eligible for a burial flag are Veterans who were entitled to retired pay for service in the Reserves or National Guard or would have been entitled if over age 60; and members or former members of the Selected Reserve who served their initial obligation or were discharged for a disability incurred or aggravated in the line of duty; or died while a member of the Selected Reserve. The next of kin may apply for the burial flag at any VA Regional Office or U.S.

88 | Burial and Memorial Benefits

Post Office by completing *VA Form 27-2008, Application for United States Flag for Burial Purposes*. In most cases, a funeral director will help the family obtain the flag. For more information, visit www. cem.va.gov/cem/burial_benefits/burial_flags.asp.

Service-Connected Burial Allowance: VA will pay a burial and funeral allowance up to $2,000 if the Veteran's death is service-connected. In such cases, the person who bore the Veteran's burial expenses may claim reimbursement from VA. There is no time limit for filing reimbursement claims in service-connected death cases. Claimants may use the *VA Form 21P-530EZ Application for Burial Benefits* to apply for benefits. There is no time limit for filing reimbursement claims in service-connected death cases.

Non-Service-Connected Burial Allowance: VA will pay a burial allowance of up to $948 for Veterans who, at the time of death from nonservice- connected injuries, were entitled to receive pension or compensation or would have been entitled if they were not receiving military retirement pay. VA will pay a burial and funeral allowance up to $948 when the Veteran's death occurs in a VA facility, a VA-contracted nursing home or a state Veterans nursing home. In cases in which the Veteran's death was not service-connected, claims must be filed within two years after burial or cremation. Claimants may use the *VA Form 21P-530EZ Application for Burial Benefits* to apply for benefits.

Plot Allowance: VA will pay a plot allowance of up to $948 when a Veteran is buried in a cemetery not under U.S. government jurisdiction if:

- the Veteran was discharged from active duty because of disability incurred or aggravated in the line of duty;
- the Veteran was receiving compensation or pension or would have been if the Veteran was not receiving military retirement pay; or
- the Veteran died in a VA facility.

The plot allowance may be paid to the state for the cost of a plot or interment in a state-owned cemetery reserved solely for Veteran burials if the Veteran is buried without charge. Burial expenses paid by the deceased's employer, or a state agency will not be reimbursed. Claimants may use the *VA Form 21P-530EZ Application for Burial Benefits* to apply for benefits.

Transportation Benefit: In some cases, VA would pay the cost of transporting the remains of a Veteran from the place of death to the place of burial if the Veteran died while hospitalized by VA or other facility listed in 38 CFR 3.1706, the Veteran's remains are unclaimed, or at the time of death, the Veteran was in receipt of disability compensation, military retired pay in lieu of disability compensation, or VA pension. Claimants may use the *VA Form 21P-530EZ Application for Burial Benefits* to apply for benefits.

For more information about burial allowances including rate tables please visit www.va.gov/burials-memorials/veterans-burial-allowance.

Outer Burial Receptacle Allowance: VA will pay a monetary allowance for an outer burial receptacle for any interment in a VA national cemetery where a privately purchased outer burial receptacle (grave liner, burial vault, or other similar container for a casket) has been used in lieu of a government-furnished grave liner. The allowance amount changes each year based on average costs and was $411 for burials that occurred in calendar year 2024.

Veterans Legacy Memorial (VLM): The VLM website, www.va.gov/remember, is the Nation's first digital platform dedicated to the memory of nearly 10 million Veterans interred in VA's national cemeteries; VA-funded state, tribal, and territory cemeteries; DOD-managed cemeteries; National Park Service cemeteries; and private cemeteries within and outside the United States. VLM Veterans represent all U.S. war and conflict periods and go back as far as the Revolutionary War.

VLM pages are automatically populated with birth and death dates (when known), military service information, and Veteran resting place details. Family, friends, and others can post tributes, images, documents, and other biographical information to a Veteran's profile page. Users can share Veteran pages using email, Facebook, and X; and can also "follow" a Veteran's page to get email alerts when new content is posted.

90 | Burial and Memorial Benefits

Veterans Cemeteries Administered by Other Agencies: The Department of the Army administers Arlington National Cemetery and other Army installation cemeteries. Eligibility is generally more restrictive than at VA national cemeteries. For information, call 703-607-8000; visit www.arlingtoncemetery.mil/about, or write:

Superintendent
Arlington National Cemetery
Arlington, VA 22211; or visit

The Department of the Interior's National Park Service maintains 14 national cemeteries located within larger park units. To view a list that includes overviews of these cemeteries, visit www.cem.va.gov/cems/ doi.asp. Andersonville National Cemetery in Andersonville, Georgia, is the only one of these 14 cemeteries that is open to new interments within the national park boundaries. For more information, call 202-208-4747, or write:

U.S. Department of the Interior National Park Service
1849 C Street, NW
Washington, DC 20240

State and Tribal Veterans Cemeteries: There are currently 122 VA grant-funded Veterans' cemeteries operating in 47 states, tribal organizations, and three U.S. Territories that offer burial options for Veterans and their families. VA grant-funded cemeteries have similar eligibility requirements to VA, though Certain states and tribal organizations may require state residency or tribal membership. Some services, particularly for family members, may require a fee. Contact the state, territorial, or tribal Veterans cemetery, or the state Veterans Affairs office for information. To locate a state, territorial or tribal Veterans cemetery, visit www.cem.va.gov/cem/grants/index.asp.

Unclaimed Veteran Remains: "Unclaimed Veterans" occur when Veterans pass away and are not claimed by relatives, friends, and/or a legal representative. In addition to burial in a VA national, VA-funded state, territorial, or tribal Veterans cemetery, and a government headstone or marker, there are monetary benefits associated with burial of unclaimed Veterans remains. These monetary benefits include reimbursement for the cost of the casket or urn used for burial, reimbursement for transportation

Burial and Memorial Benefits | 91

to a national, state, or tribal Veterans cemetery, and a burial allowance and plot allowance. Learn more at www.cem.va.gov/facts/Unclaimed_Veteran_Remains.asp and www.benefits.va.gov/persona/indigent-veterans-unclaimed-remains.asp. Applicants must submit *VA Form 40-10088, Request for Reimbursement of Casket/Urn*. For Veterans who die while at a VA facility under authorized VA admission or at a non-VA facility under authorized VA admission and are unclaimed, the closest VA healthcare facility is responsible for arranging proper burial for the unclaimed Veteran.

Additional Benefits

Veterans and Survivors Needing Fiduciary Services: The fiduciary program provides oversight of VA's most vulnerable beneficiaries who are unable to manage their VA benefits because of injury, disease, the infirmities of advanced age, or being under 18 years of age. VA closely monitors fiduciaries for compliance with program responsibilities to ensure that VA benefits are being used to meet the needs, security, and comfort of beneficiaries and their dependents. In deciding who should act as fiduciary for a beneficiary, VA will always select the most effective and least restrictive fiduciary arrangement. For more information about VA's fiduciary program, please visit our website at www.benefits. va.gov/fiduciary/index.asp.

VA Benefits for Veterans Living Overseas: VA monetary benefits, including disability compensation, pension, educational benefits, and burial allowances, are generally payable overseas. Some programs are restricted. Home loan guaranties are available only in the U.S. Educational benefits are limited to approved, degree granting programs in institutions of higher learning. Beneficiaries living in foreign countries should contact the nearest American embassy or consulate for help. In Canada, contact an office of VA. For information, visit www.benefits.va.gov/persona/veteran-abroad.asp.

Incarcerated Veterans: VA service-connected disability compensation benefits are affected if a Veteran is convicted of a felony and incarcerated for more than 60 days. VA pension benefits are affected if a Veteran or beneficiary is convicted of a felony or misdemeanor and incarcerated for more than 60 days. Disability compensation paid to an incarcerated Veteran rated 20% or more disabled is limited to the 10% rate. For a Veteran whose disability rating is 10%, the payment is reduced to half of the rate payable to a Veteran evaluated as 10% disabled. Payments are not reduced for participants in work-release programs, residing in halfway houses or under community control. Disability, death, or survivor pension paid to a Veteran or beneficiary incarcerated following conviction of a felony or misdemeanor must be discontinued.

Benefits not paid to a Veteran or surviving spouse while incarcerated may be apportioned to eligible dependents. Failure to notify VA of a Veteran or beneficiary's incarceration can result in overpayment of benefits and the subsequent loss of all VA financial benefits until the overpayment is recovered.

NOTE: VA benefits will not be provided to any Veteran, survivor or dependent wanted for an outstanding felony warrant. Failure to notify VA of a Veteran or beneficiary's incarceration can result in overpayment of benefits and the subsequent loss of all VA financial benefits until the overpayment is recovered.

For more information, visit www.benefits.va.gov/persona/veteran-incarcerated.asp.

The Health Care for Re-Entry Veterans (HCRV) Program: The HCRV program is designed to address the needs of incarcerated Veterans when re-entering their community. The goals of HCRV are to prevent homelessness; reduce the impact of medical, psychiatric and substance use problems on community readjustment; and decrease the likelihood of re-incarceration for those leaving prison. To locate an outreach worker, visit www.va.gov/homeless/reentry.asp.

The Veterans Justice Outreach Program: The purpose of the Veterans Justice Outreach program is to prevent homelessness and avoid the unnecessary criminalization of mental illness and extended incarceration among Veterans. This is accomplished by ensuring that eligible justice-involved Veterans encountered by police and in jails or courts, have timely access to VHA mental health, substance use, and homeless services when clinically indicated, and other VA services and benefits as appropriate. To locate a Veterans Justice Outreach Specialist, please visit www.va.gov/homeless/vjo.asp.

Also, within the Veterans Justice Programs, the new Legal Services for Veterans (LSV) program will administer grants to eligible organizations for the provision of certain legal services to homeless and at-risk Veterans. The first LSV grants will be awarded in FY 2023. For more information, visit www.va.gov/HOMELESS/lsv.asp.

Service members Transitioning from the Military: VA has personnel assigned to major military hospitals and DoD installations to help wounded, ill and injured Service members transition from military to civilian life. VA Liaisons for Healthcare are available at every military installation and provide individualized assistance connecting to VA health care. More information about what to expect from the VA Liaisons for Healthcare as well as their contact information is available at www.va.gov/POST911VETERANS/VA_Liaison_Program.asp.

Service members who have questions about VA benefits or need assistance filing a VA claim or accessing services, can contact the nearest VA office, call 800-827-1000, or 1-800-MyVA411 (800-698-2411), option 5.

VOW to Hire Heroes Act: The Act made the Transition Assistance Program (TAP), including attendance at VA benefit briefings, mandatory for most Service members transitioning to civilian status; upgraded career counseling options; focused TAP more heavily on job hunting skills; and tailored the program for the 21st century job market. The Act allows Service members to begin the post-military employment process prior to separation or retirement from military service. It also provides disabled Veterans up to one year of additional VR&E benefits. The Act provides tax credits for hiring Veterans and disabled Veterans who are out of work.

Transition Assistance Program (TAP): TAP is an interagency program designed to provide Service members with benefits and service information to ease their transition from military to civilian life. The program is supported by the Department of Defense (DoD), Department of Labor (DOL), Department of Education (DoE), Department of Veteran Affairs (VA), Department of Homeland Security (DHS), Small Business Administration (SBA) and the Office of Personnel Management (OPM). Service members who are retiring can participate in TAP as early as two years prior to retirement. However, all transitioning Service members (separatees and retirees) must participate in TAP no later than one year prior to separation or retirement. The TAP curriculum provides the skill building, resources, and tools Service members need to achieve emotional health, physical health, and economic stability in civilian life.

The VA portion of TAP is a one-day in-person, virtual instructor-led, or online course called VA Benefits and Services. The course

Additional Benefits | 95

offers interactive exercises and real-life examples to help Service members navigate VA and the benefits and services they have earned through their military careers. It covers topics like family support, disability compensation, education, and health care benefits. Service members can also access the virtual TAP curriculum, including the VA Benefits and Services course, and Military Life Cycle (MLC) modules any time through Transition Online Learning at www.TAPevents.mil/courses. For more information on VA TAP, visit benefits.va.gov/transition/tap.asp.

Women's Health Transition Training: The online, self-paced Women's Health Transition Training is available for servicewomen and newly separated women Veterans to take any time, any place at www.TAPevents.mil/courses. This course provides important information for transitioning servicewomen on women's health care services available from VA post-separation from the military.

***in*Transition Program:** *in*Transition is a free, voluntary program with coaches who provide psychological health care support to Service members, Veterans, and their health care providers during times of transition. This program provides access to transitional support, motivation and healthy lifestyle assistance, and advice from qualified coaches through the toll-free telephone number 800-424-7877. For more information, visit health.mil/Military-Health-Topics/Centers-of-Excellence/Psychological-Health-Center-of-Excellence/inTransition.

Pre-Separation Counseling through Military Service: Service members may receive pre-separation counseling 24 months prior to retirement or 12 months prior to separation from active duty. These sessions present information on education, training, employment assistance, National Guard and Reserve programs, medical benefits, and financial assistance.

Verification of Military Experience and Training (VMET): The VMET Document, DD Form 2586, helps Service members verify previous experience and training to potential employers, negotiate credits at schools, and obtain certificates or licenses. VMET documents are available only through each military branch's support office and are intended for Service members who have at least six months of active duty. Service members should obtain

96 | Additional Benefits

VMET documents from their Transition Support Office within 12 months of separation or 24 months of retirement.

Veterans' Workforce Investment Program: Recently separated Veterans and those with service-connected disabilities, significant barriers to employment, or who served on active duty during a period in which a campaign or expedition badge was authorized, can contact the nearest state employment office for employment help through the Veterans Workforce Investment Program. The program may be conducted through state or local public agencies, community organizations or private, non-profit organizations.

Veterans Employment Services: VA's Veteran and Military Spouse Talent Engagement Program (VMSTEP): VMSTEP provides guidance, and assistance to Veterans and military spouses seeking employment in the U.S. Department of Veterans Affairs. Part of the services they provide include teaching Veterans how to maximize their military skills to match the Department's critical staffing needs. VMSTEP helps Veterans and military spouses understand the Federal hiring process through virtual training opportunities such as writing your Federal resume, navigating through www.usajobs.gov, and interviewing for jobs. VMSTEP advocates and brings awareness of the Department's military spouse employment opportunities and Veteran Employment Initiatives specifically designed for disabled Veterans to increase employment opportunities. For more information, please visit www.vaforvets.va.gov and follow us on Facebook at www.facebook.com/VMSTEP.VAforVets.

State Employment Services: Veterans can find employment information, education and training opportunities, job counseling, job search workshops, and resume preparation assistance by visiting their individual State Departments of Veteran Affairs. Many states have Veterans Employment Centers at state Workforce Career or One-Stop Centers. These offices also have specialists to help disabled Veterans find employment. Additional information and access to services are available at www.va.gov/careers-employment/.

Unemployment Compensation: Veterans who do not begin civilian employment immediately after leaving military service

Additional Benefits | 97

may receive weekly unemployment compensation for a limited time. The amount and duration of payments are determined by individual states. Apply by contacting the nearest state employment office listed in the local telephone directory.

Veterans Preference for Federal Jobs: Since the time of the Civil War, Veterans of the Armed Forces have been given some degree of preference in appointments to federal jobs.

Veterans' preference in its present form comes from the Veterans' Preference Act of 1944, as amended, and now codified in Title 5, U.S.C. By law, Veterans who are disabled or who served on active duty during certain specified time periods or in military campaigns are entitled to preference over others when hiring from competitive lists of eligible candidates and in retention during a reduction in force.

To receive preference, a Veteran must have been discharged or released from active duty under honorable conditions or received a general discharge. Preference is also provided for certain widows and widowers of Veterans who died in service, spouses of service-connected disabled Veterans, and mothers of Veterans who died under honorable conditions on active duty or have permanent and total service-connected disabilities.

Enrolled Veterans can print a copy of their preference letter from the VA.gov portal. For more information about Veterans Preference, please visit www.va.gov/careers-employment.

Veterans' Recruitment Appointment: Veterans' recruitment appointment allows federal agencies to appoint eligible Veterans to jobs without competition. These appointments can be converted to career or career-conditional positions after two years of satisfactory work. Veterans should apply directly to the agency where they wish to work. For additional information on Veterans Recruitment Appointment, visit www.va.gov/careers-employment.

Small Businesses: The Small Business Administration (SBA) certifies Service-Disabled Veteran-Owned and Veteran-Owned firms seeking to do business within VA's Veterans First

Contracting Program. For additional information visit veterans.certify.sba.gov.

VA's Office of Small & Disadvantaged Business Utilization (OSDBU) offers no-cost resources to help Service-Disabled Veteran-Owned Small Businesses and Veteran-Owned Small Businesses succeed in Federal contracting. With OSDBU assistance, small and disadvantaged businesses can expect to:

- Engage with Procurement Decision Makers from VA, other Government agencies, and private industry to learn best practices for doing business with Government entities, to specifically include VA;
- Network and form relationships with large, small, and disadvantaged businesses for potential teaming and partnership opportunities;
- Attend educational small business community outreach events to learn about VA opportunities and programs;
- Participate in small business training webinars, and access our training library available across several platforms, including the OSDBU website, LinkedIn, and YouTube;
- Engage with VA Small Business Liaisons to learn about local and regional contracting opportunities; and
- Explore strategic partnership opportunities.

Low Income Home Energy Assistance Program (LIHEAP): The U.S. Department of Health and Human Services provides funding to states to help low-income households with their heating and home energy costs under LIHEAP. LIHEAP can also assist with insulating homes to make them more energy efficient and reduce energy costs. The LIHEAP program in each community determines if your household's income qualifies for the program. To find out where to apply, call 866-674-6327 between 7 a.m. - 5 p.m. MT or e-mail energy@ncat.org. More information can be found at www.acf.hhs.gov/ocs/programs/liheap.

Achieving a Better Life Experience Act (ABLE): ABLE became law on December 19, 2014. The law aims to ease financial strains faced by individuals with disabilities by making tax-free saving accounts

Additional Benefits | 99

available to cover qualified disability expenses. The designated beneficiary of an ABLE account is the eligible individual who owns the ABLE account. They must be:

- Eligible for Supplemental Security Income (SSI) based on disability or blindness that began before age 26; or

- Entitled to disability insurance benefits, childhood disability benefits or disabled widow's or widower's benefits based on disability or blindness that began before age 26; or

- Someone who has certified (or whose parent or guardian has certified) that they have met the criteria for a disability certification before age 26.

For more information on ABLE accounts, see Internal Revenue Service Publication 907, Tax Highlights for Persons With Disabilities at www.irs.gov/pub/irs-pdf/p907.pdf and the Social Security Administration spotlight on achieving a better life experience at www.ssa.gov/ssi/spotlights/spot-able.html.

NOTES

NOTES

NOTES